Lecture Notes in Artificial Intelligence 10399

Subseries of Lecture Notes in Computer Science

More information about this series at http://www.springer.com/series/1244

Luis Gustavo Nardin · Luis Antunes (Eds.)

Multi-Agent Based Simulation XVII

International Workshop, MABS 2016
Singapore, Singapore, May 10, 2016
Revised Selected Papers

Springer

Editors
Luis Gustavo Nardin
Center for Modeling Complex Interactions
University of Idaho
Moscow, ID
USA

Luis Antunes
GUESS/BioISI, Faculdade de Ciências
Universidade de Lisboa
Lisbon
Portugal

ISSN 0302-9743 ISSN 1611-3349 (electronic)
Lecture Notes in Artificial Intelligence
ISBN 978-3-319-67476-6 ISBN 978-3-319-67477-3 (eBook)
DOI 10.1007/978-3-319-67477-3

Library of Congress Control Number: 2017953436

LNCS Sublibrary: SL7 – Artificial Intelligence

Printed on acid-free paper

This Springer imprint is published by Springer Nature
The registered company is Springer International Publishing AG
The registered company address is: Gewerbestrasse 11, 6330 Cham, Switzerland

Preface

The Multi-Agent-Based Simulation (MABS) workshop series aims to bring together researchers engaged in modeling and in analyzing multi-agent systems, and those interested in applying agent-based simulation techniques to real-world problems. Its scientific focus lies in the confluence of socio-technical-natural sciences and multi-agent systems, with a strong application/empirical vein. Lately, its emphasis has been placed on (i) exploratory agent-based simulation as a principled way of undertaking scientific research in the social sciences, and (ii) using social theories as an inspiration to new frameworks and developments in multi-agent systems.

The 2016 International Multi-Agent-Based Simulation workshop was held in conjunction with the 15th Autonomous Agents and Multi-Agent Systems conference (AAMAS) in Singapore in May 2016. This volume represents the 17th in a series that began in 1998. Fifteen papers from 10 countries were submitted to the workshop. We selected 10 papers for presentation (around 66% acceptance). The papers presented at the workshop were extended, revised, and re-reviewed, incorporating points from the discussions held at the workshop with their original ideas. In this MABS edition, two papers, the most "visionary" and the "best" papers, had already been published by Springer in the Lecture Notes in Artificial Intelligence (LNAI) series and the Communications in Computer and Information Science (CCIS) series, respectively.

The workshop could not have taken place without the contribution of many people. We are very grateful to Virginia Dignum, who gave a very inspiring invited talk, and to all the participants, who took part in a lively debate during the presentation of the papers. We are also very grateful to all the members of the Program Committee for their hard work. Thanks are also due to Carles Sierra and Nardine Osman (AAMAS 2016 workshop chairs), to Stacy Marsella and Catholijn Jonker (AAMAS 2016 general co-chairs), to John Thangarajah and Karl Tuyls (AAMAS 2016 program co-chairs), and to Pradeep Varakantham (AAMAS 2016 local arrangements chair).

June 2017
Luis Gustavo Nardin
Luis Antunes

Organization

General and Program Chairs

Luis Gustavo Nardin University of Idaho, USA
Luis Antunes University of Lisbon, Portugal

MABS Steering Committee

Frédéric Amblard Université Toulouse 1 Capitole, France
Luis Antunes University of Lisbon, Portugal
Rosaria Conte ISTC–National Research Council, Italy
Paul Davidsson Malmö University, Sweden
Nigel Gilbert University of Surrey, UK
Scott Moss University of Koblenz-Landau, Germany
Keith Sawyer University of North Carolina, USA
Jaime Simão Sichman University of São Paulo, Brazil
Keiki Takadama University of Electro-Communications, Japan

Program Committee

Frédéric Amblard Université Toulouse 1 Capitole, France
Luis Antunes University of Lisbon, Portugal
Robert Axtell George Mason University, USA
João Balsa University of Lisbon, Portugal
Ana Bazzan Federal University of Rio Grande do Sul, Brazil
Tibor Bosse Vrije Universiteit Amsterdam, Netherlands
Cristiano Castelfranchi ISTC–National Research Council, Italy
Shu-Heng Chen National Chengchi University, Taiwan
Sung-Bae Cho Yonsei University, South Korea
Helder Coelho University of Lisbon, Portugal
Rosaria Conte ISTC–National Research Council, Italy
Paul Davidsson Malmö University, Sweden
Gennaro Di Tosto Ohio State University, USA
Frank Dignum Utrecht University, Netherlands
Virginia Dignum TU Delft, Netherlands
Alexis Drogoul IRD, Vietnam
Bruce Edmonds Manchester Metropolitan University, UK
Benoit Gaudou Université Toulouse 1 Capitole, France
Nick Gotts Independent Researcher, UK
László Gulyás AITIA International Inc., Hungary
Rainer Hegselmann University of Bayreuth, Germany
Wander Jager University of Gröningen, Netherlands

Marco Janssen	Arizona State University, USA
William Kennedy	George Mason University, USA
Satoshi Kurihara	University of Electro-Communications, Japan
Ulf Lotzmann	University of Koblenz-Landau, Germany
Ruth Meyer	Manchester Metropolitan University, UK
Jean-Pierre Müller	CIRAD, France
John Murphy	Argonne National Laboratory, USA
Emma Norling	Manchester Metropolitan University, UK
Michael North	Argonne National Laboratory, USA
Paulo Novais	University of Minho, Portugal
Mario Paolucci	ISTC–National Research Council, Italy
Juan Pavón	Universidad Complutense de Madrid, Spain
William Rand	University of Maryland, USA
Keith Sawyer	University of North Carolina, USA
Jeffrey Schank	University of California Davis, USA
Jaime Sichman	University of São Paulo, Brazil
Carles Sierra	IIIA, Spain
Flaminio Squazzoni	University of Brescia, Italy
Keiki Takadama	University of Electro-Communications, Japan
Takao Terano	Tokyo Institute of Technology, Japan
Dilhan Thilakarathne	Vrije Universiteit Amsterdam, Netherlands
Jan Treur	Vrije Universiteit Amsterdam, Netherlands
Klaus Troitzsch	University of Koblenz-Landau, Germany
Stephen Turner	Nanyang Technological University, Singapore
Harko Verhagen	Stockholm University, Sweden
Gerard Weisbuch	École Normale Supérieure, France

Contents

Architectures, Methods and Methodologies

A BDI Agent Architecture for the GAMA Modeling and Simulation Platform

Patrick Taillandier[1][✉], Mathieu Bourgais[1,2], Philippe Caillou[3], Carole Adam[4], and Benoit Gaudou[5]

[1] MIAT, University of Toulouse, INRA, Toulouse, Castanet-Tolosan, France
patrick.taillandier@gmail.com, mathieu.bourgais@insa-rouen.fr
[2] EA 4108 LITIS, INSA of Rouen, Rouen, France
[3] UMR 8623 LRI, University of Paris Sud, Paris, France
caillou@lri.fr
[4] UMR 5217 LIG, University of Grenoble, Grenoble, France
carole.adam@imag.fr
[5] UMR 5505 IRIT, University of Toulouse, Toulouse, France
benoit.gaudou@ut-capitole.fr

Abstract. With the increase of computing power and the development of user-friendly multi-agent simulation frameworks, social simulations have become increasingly realistic. However, most agent architectures in these simulations use simple reactive models. Indeed, cognitive agent architectures face two main obstacles: their complexity for the field-expert modeler, and their computational cost. In this paper, we propose a new cognitive agent architecture based on the BDI (Belief-Desire-Intention) paradigm integrated into the GAMA modeling platform and its GAML modeling language. This architecture was designed to be simple-to-use for modelers, flexible enough to manage complex behaviors, and with low computational cost. An experiment carried out with different profiles of end-users shows that the architecture is actually usable even by modelers who have little knowledge in programming and in Artificial Intelligence.

Keywords: Agent-based simulation · BDI architecture · GAMA platform

1 Introduction

Agent-based simulations are widely used to study complex systems. When the goal is to understand or even predict the behaviour of such complex systems, the simulation requires an accurate agent architecture to lay valid results. However, designing the agents is still an open issue, especially for models in social simulations, where some of the agents represent human beings. In fact, designing complex agents able to act in a believable way is a difficult task, in particular when their behaviour is led by many conflicting needs and desires.

© Springer International Publishing AG 2017
L.G. Nardin and L. Antunes (Eds.): MABS 2016, LNAI 10399, pp. 3–23, 2017.
DOI: 10.1007/978-3-319-67477-3_1

A classic paradigm to formalize the internal architecture of such complex agents in Agent-Oriented Software Engineering is the BDI (Belief-Desire-Intention) paradigm. This paradigm, based on the philosophy of action [7], allows to design expressive and realistic agents, yet it is still rarely used in social simulations, for two main reasons [3]. First, most agent architectures based on the BDI paradigm are too complex to be understood and used by non-computer-scientists. Second, they are often very time-consuming in terms of computation and therefore not adapted to simulations with thousands of agents.

In a previous paper [8], we proposed a first architecture to overcome these obstacles. This architecture is now fully integrated into the GAMA platform, an open-source modeling and simulation platform for building spatially explicit agent-based simulations [2,10,11]. GAMA's Modeling Language (GAML) and the integrated development environment support the definition of large scale models (up to millions of agents) and are usable even with low-level programming skills. Our BDI architecture was implemented as a new GAMA plug-in, and enables the straightforward definition of BDI agents through the GAML language. Thus, modelers have a wide range of ways to define their agents behaviors, by mixing classic GAMA primitives with BDI concepts. Indeed, we state that there is no unique way of defining the behavior of agents that can fit all the possible application contexts, types of agents to define (level of cognition), and modelers' backgrounds (programming skills, modeling habits...).

This paper describes some major improvements for the architecture, as well as a usability study carried out with modelers. The paper is structured as follows: Sect. 2 proposes a state of the art of BDI architectures and their use in simulations. Section 3 is dedicated to the presentation of our architecture, and more particularly the novelties from our previous work. In Sect. 4, we present an experiment in which we asked modelers with different profiles to test the architecture. Finally, Sect. 5 provides a conclusion and some perspectives.

2   State of the Art

2.1   Agent Architectures for Social Simulations

Balke and Gilbert [4] cite Sun as remarking that "social simulation researchers frequently only focus on agent models custom-tailored to the task at hand. He calls this situation unsatisfying and emphasises that it limits realism and the applicability of social simulation. He argues that to overcome these shortcomings, it is necessary to include cognition as an integral part of an agent architecture." There are several options to endow agents with complex cognitive capabilities: cognitive architectures based on cognitive sciences, such as SOAR or ACT-R, or BDI architectures based on the philosophy of action.

2.2   BDI Agents in AOSE Frameworks

The BDI approach has been proposed in Artificial Intelligence [7] to represent the way agents can do complex reasoning. It has first been formalized using

Modal Logic [9] in order to disambiguate the BDI concepts (Belief, Desire and Intention; detailed in Sect. 3.1) and the logical relationships between them.

In parallel, the Agent-Oriented Software Engineering (AOSE) field designed BDI operational architectures to help the development of Multi-Agent Systems embedding BDI agents. Some of these BDI architectures are included in frameworks allowing to directly use them in different applications. A classic framework is the Procedural Reasoning System (PRS) [14], that has been used as a base for many other frameworks (commercial, *e.g.* JACK [12], or open-source, *e.g.* JADE [6] with its add-on Jadex [15] offering an explicit representation of goals).

2.3   BDI Agents in ABMS Platforms

BDI architectures have been introduced in several agent-based modelling and simulation (ABMS) platforms. For example, Sakellariou et al. [17] have proposed an education-oriented extension to Netlogo [20] to allow modellers to manipulate BDI concepts in a simple language. This very simple architecture is inspired by PRS: agents have a set of beliefs (information obtained by perception or communication), a set of intentions (what they want to execute), and ways to manage these two sets.

Singh and Padgham [18] went one step further by proposing a framework acting like a middleware to connect components such as an ABMS platform and a BDI framework (*e.g.* JACK [12] or Jadex [15]). They demonstrated their framework on an application coupling the Matsim platform [5] and the GORITE BDI framework [16] for a bushfire simulation. Their framework aims at being generic and can be extended to couple any kind of ABMS platforms and BDI frameworks, only by implementing interfaces to plug each new component to the middleware. This approach is very powerful but remains computer-scientist-oriented, as it requires high programming skills to develop bridges for each component and to implement agents behaviours without a dedicated modelling language.

2.4   Previous Work: BDI Agents in GAMA

First attempts already exist to integrate BDI agents into the GAMA platform [11]. Taillandier et al. [19] proposed a BDI architecture where the choice of plans is formalized as a multi-criteria decision-making process: desires are represented as criteria, and decisions are made by evaluating each plan *w.r.t.* each criterion according to the agent's beliefs. However, this architecture was tightly linked to its application context (farmer's decision making), did not offer any formalism to model the agent's beliefs, and was rather limited *w.r.t.* how plans were carried out (*e.g.* no possibility to have complex plans with sub-objectives).

Le et al. [13] proposed another architecture dedicated to simulation with a formalized description of beliefs and plans and their execution. However, the desires and plans have to be written in a very specific and complex way that can be difficult to achieve for some application contexts, in particular for non-computer scientists. In addition, this architecture has a scalability problem: it does not allow to simulate thousands of agents.

Finally, we proposed in [8] a first simple architecture. This generic architecture proved its interest through an application to simulate agricultural parcels dynamics in Vietnam. However, the use of this architecture required to write many lines of code, in particular to manage the perceptions of agents and the inference of desires. Moreover, it did not allow to manage plans with different temporal scales. All these limitations made this architecture not usable for some applications and more complex to use by non-computer scientists. The next section therefore presents the improvements that we performed on this architecture.

3   Presentation of the Architecture

3.1   Overview

Our architecture is defined as a GAMA species architecture. The modeler is only required to define *simpleBDI* as the agent's architecture, and to define at least one plan and one initial desire to make it operational. The modeler then mostly defines plans (what the agent can do), desires (what the agent wants) and (usually one) perception(s) (how the agent perceives its environment). Many keywords and functions are defined to help the user updating and managing Beliefs, Desires and Intentions bases, and creating and managing predicates.

The architecture and the vocabulary can be summarized with this simple Gold Miner example: the Miner agent has a general *desire* to find gold. As it is the only thing it wants at the beginning, it is its initial *intention* (what it is currently doing). To find gold, it wanders around (its *plan* is to wander). When it *perceives* some gold nuggets, it stores this information (it has a new *belief* about the existence and location of this gold nugget), and it adopts a new *desire* (it wants to extract this gold). When it perceives a gold nugget, the *intention* to find gold is put *on hold* and a new *intention* is selected (to extract gold). To achieve this *intention*, the *plan* has two steps, *i.e.* two new *(sub)intentions*: to choose a gold nugget to extract (among its known gold nuggets) and to go and take it. And so on.

This vocabulary is explained in more details in the next section.

3.2   Vocabulary

Knowledge. Beliefs, Desires and Intentions are described using **predicates**. A predicate has a name, it may also have values (a set of name-value pairs), and can be true (by default) or false. Predicates can be easily defined through the GAML language. For example, in Fig. 1, we define a new predicate *location_gold*, that represents the fact that a gold nugget is present at location (20, 50). Note that when comparing two predicates, if one of them has no value for a specific key, the values corresponding to this key are not considered. For instance, testing if the predicate ("location_gold") is present in the belief base will return true if the predicate ("location_gold", ["location_value" :: 20, 50]) is in the base (or the same predicate with any other value).

```
new_predicate("location_gold",["location_value"::{20,50}]);
```

Fig. 1. Predicate definition

BDI agents have 3 databases:

- **belief_base** (what it knows): the internal knowledge the agent has about the world or about its internal state, updated during the simulation. A belief can concern any type of information (a quantity, a location, a boolean value, etc.) and is described by a predicate. For example the predicate *gold_location* (Fig. 1) is added as a belief when the agent perceives a gold nugget at position (20,50).
- **desire_base** (what it wants): objectives that the agent would like to accomplish, also updated during the simulation. A desire is fulfilled when it is present in the Belief base (for example if I desire that the gold nugget at a certain location no longer exists in the world, and I also believe this to be true, then my desire is fulfilled and is removed from my desire base) or when it is removed by the agent. Desires can have hierarchical links (**sub/super desires**) when a desire is created as an intermediary objective. Desires have a dynamic **priority** value used to select a new intention among the desires when necessary.
- **intention_base** (what it is doing): what the agent has chosen to do. The **current intention** will determine the selected plan. Intentions can be put **on hold** (for example when they require a sub-intention to be achieved). For this reason, there is a stack of intentions: the top one is the current intention, all others are on hold.

Behavior. In addition to the basic behavior structures available for all GAMA agents, our *simpleBDI* architecture has three available types of behavior structures (which are new compared to [8]):

- **Perception:** A perception is a function executed at each iteration to update the agent's Belief base, to observe the changes in its environment (the world, the other agents and itself). The agent can perceive other agents up to a fixed distance or inside a specific geometry. For example, a miner can perceive all the gold nuggets at a distance of 10 m and for each of them add a new belief concerning the gold's location (see Fig. 2). Like for many other GAMA statements, several facets (most of them optional) can be used to tune the perceptions:
    - **target** (mandatory): the list of agents (or species of agents) to perceive.
    - **when** (optional): perception condition - can be a dynamic expression.
    - **in** (optional): can be either a radius (float) or a geometry (for instance, definition of a cone of perception or something more complex).
- **Rule:** A rule is a function executed at each iteration to infer new desires or beliefs from the agent's current beliefs and desires, i.e. a new desire or belief

can emerge from the existing ones. For example, when the miner has a belief about some gold nuggets at a specific location, the rule creates the desire to extract gold (see Fig. 3). Of course, if the new desire (or belief) is already in the base, nothing is added. Rules facets are the following:

- **belief** (optional): required belief to activate the rule.
- **desire** (optional): required desire to activate the rule.
- **when** (optional): required condition to activate the rule.
- **new_belief** (optional): the new belief to be added to the agent's base.
- **new_desire** (optional): the new desire to be added to the agent's base.

- **Plan:** The agent has a set of **plans**, which are behaviors defined to accomplish specific intentions. Plans can be instantaneous and/or persistent, and may have a **priority** value (that can be dynamic), used to select a plan when several possible plans are available to accomplish the same intention. For example, when the miner has the intention to $find\_gold$, it can activate its $letsWander$ plan (see Fig. 4) that makes it randomly move. Concerning the facets of plans:
  - **intention** (optional): intention the plan try to fulfill.
  - **when** (optional): activation condition.
  - **finished_when** (optional): termination condition.
  - **priority** (optional): priority of the plan, 1 by default.
  - **instantaneous** (optional): if $false$, no other plan can be executed afterwards during the current simulation step; otherwise, (at least) one other plan will be executed during the same step. By default $false$.

```
perceive target:gold in:10 {
    focus var:location;
}
```

Fig. 2. Perception definition: when the agent perceives a gold nugget at a distance lower than 10 m, a new belief is added concerning the location of this gold nugget.

```
rule belief: new_predicate("location_gold") new_desire: get_gold ;
```

Fig. 3. Rule definition: when the agent has a belief about a gold nugget somewhere, a desire is added to extract gold

3.3   Thinking Process

At each step, the agent applies the process described in Fig. 5. Roughly, the agent first perceives the environment, then (i) **continues its current plan** if it is not finished, or (ii) if the plan is finished and its current intention is not fulfilled, it **selects a new plan**, or (iii) if its current intention is fulfilled, it **selects a new desire** to add to its intention stack.

```
plan letsWander intention:find_gold {
    do wander;
}
```

Fig. 4. Plan definition: if the agent has the intention to *find_gold*, it can use the *letsWander* plan, which makes the agent moves randomly (uses of the *wander* built-in action of GAMA)

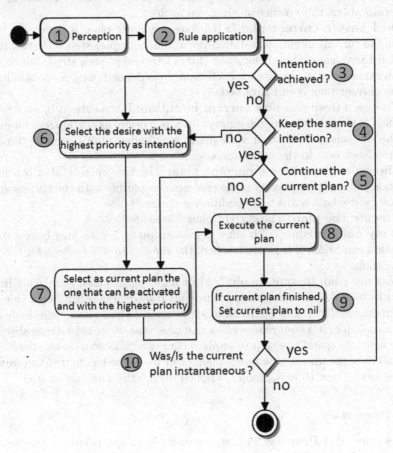

Fig. 5. Activity diagram

This process is similar to the one proposed in [8], however it introduces the perception and rule steps. In addition, it allows to apply several plans in the same time step in case of instantaneous plans. More precisely (see Activity Diagram in Fig. 5).

1. **Perceive:** Perceptions are executed.
2. **Rule:** Rules are executed.

3. **Is one of my intentions achieved?:** If one of my intentions is achieved, sets the current plan to nil and removes the intention and all its sub-desires from the desire and intention bases. If the achieved intention's super-desire is on hold, it is reactivated (since its sub-desire just got completed).
4. **Do I keep the current intention?:** To take into account the environment instability, an intention-persistence coefficient ip is applied: with the probability ip, the current intention is removed from the intention stack. More details about this coefficient are given in Sect. 3.4.
5. **Do I have a current plan?:** If I have a current plan, just execute it. As for the current intention stability, the aim is both persistence (I stick to the plan I have chosen) and efficiency (I don't choose at each step). Similarly to intentions, a plan-persistence coefficient pp is defined: with a probability pp, the current plan is just dropped.
6. **Choose a desire as new current intention:** If the current intention is on hold (or the intention base is empty), choose a desire as new current intention. The new selected intention is the desire with higher priority among those not already present in the intention base.
7. **Choose a plan as new current plan:** The new current plan is selected among the highest priority plans that are compatible with the current intention (and whose activation condition is checked).
8. **Execute the plan:** The current plan is executed.
9. **Is my plan finished?:** To allow persistent plans, a plan may have a termination condition. If it is not reached, the same plan will be kept for the next iteration.
10. **Was my plan instantaneous?:** Most multi-agent based simulation frameworks (GAMA included) are synchronous frameworks using steps. One consequence is that it may be useful to apply several plans during one single step. For example, if a step represents a day or a year, it would be unrealistic for an agent to spend one step to apply a plan like "choose a destination". This kind of plans (mostly reasoning plans) can be defined as **instantaneous**: in this case a new thinking loop is applied during the same agent step.

3.4   Properties

Persistence and Priority. Persistence coefficients and priority values are key properties of many BDI architectures. Agents with high persistence continue their current actions independently of the environment evolution (they are more stable and spend less time rethinking their plans and objectives). Less persistent agents are more adaptable and reactive but may lead to erratic and computationally costly behaviors. Priority values will determine both the selected desires and plans. The choice can be deterministic (highest priority selected) or probabilistic (highest priority have a higher probability to be selected). One advantage of the GAMA modeling framework for both persistence and priority coefficients is to allow the use of dynamic or function-based variables. Plans and Desires priority values and agent persistence coefficients can be changed by the agent itself (for example, a plan could increase the persistence coefficient after evaluating the previous plan success). The modeler can also define functions to update a value. For example, the priority of a plan or desire could be defined as a function of the current step, which would make it more and more probable to be selected when the simulation advances.

Flexibility. One core objective when defining this architecture was to make it as simple-to-use and flexible as possible for the modeler. The modeler can use the architecture in its full potential (for example dynamic coefficients as presented before), but he/she can also use only some parts of the architecture. It is for example possible to define only Desires and Plans, and no Beliefs (the effect would be that the intentions and desires achievement and removal will have to be done manually, i.e. defined by the modeler in the agent plans). Most parameters have default values and can be omitted. For example, the modeler doesn't have to know the existence of instantaneous plans (by default off), plan termination condition (by default true: always terminated at the end of its execution), or the possibility to define sub-desires or put intentions on hold.

In addition, in order to manipulate the different elements of the architecture, we provide modelers with built-in actions directly usable in their models, among which (desire related actions are not listed here):

- **add_belief:** add a new belief to the belief base.
- **remove_belief:** remove a belief from the belief base.
- **has_belief:** test if a belief is in the belief base.
- **replace_belief:** replace a belief by a new one in the belief base.
- **get_belief:** return the first belief corresponding to a given predicate.
- **get_beliefs:** return all beliefs corresponding to a given predicate.
- **remove_all_beliefs:** remove all beliefs corresponding to a given predicate.
- **clear_beliefs:** remove all beliefs.
- **get_current_intention:** return the current intention.
- **clear_intentions:** remove all intentions.
- **add_subintentions:** add a sub-intentions to a predicate.
- **current_intention_on_hold:** put the current intention on hold and add as its activation condition all its sub-intentions.

3.5 A Complete Example

To illustrate our architecture with a more detailed example, we present here an implementation of the gold miner model (see Sect. 3.1). A snapshot of the model is shown in Fig. 6.

The complete model can be found on the ACTEUR Website [1].

We define 3 species of agents: **miner** (the miners), **gold** (the gold nuggets) and **base** (the base where the miners store their gold nuggets, which is unique). Due to space constraints, we only detail here the behavior of the miner agents.

The miner agents use the *simpleBDI* architecture. 8 variables are defined for this species (Fig. 7):

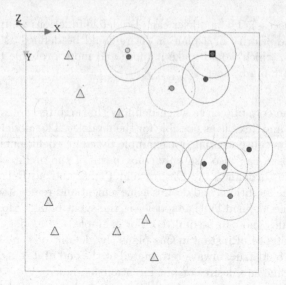

Fig. 6. Snapshot of the gold miner model: the yellow triangles are the gold nuggets, the black square is the base, and the circles are the miners. The empty circle around each miner is their perception range. (Color figure online)

- **speed:** the moving speed of the agent (3 m/s)
- **mycolor:** a random color that will be used to display the agent
- **target:** the location where the agent wants to go (only used when the agent is not wandering).
- **has_gold:** a predicate used as the belief that indicates that the agent has a gold nugget.
- **define_gold_target:** a predicate used as the desire to define a new target (with a priority value of 3).
- **get_gold:** a predicate used as the desire to take a gold nugget (with a priority value of 2).
- **wander:** a predicate used as the desire to wander.
- **return_base:** a predicate used as the desire to return to the base (with a priority value of 3).

The species uses one perception and two rules (Fig. 8):

- **perception:** the perception allows to perceive the gold nuggets in a radius of 20 m. Each time a gold nugget is perceived, a new belief concerning the location of the gold nugget is added to the belief base and the intention to wander is removed.
- **rule:** the first rule adds a new desire to take a gold nugget if the agent believes that there is a gold nugget somewhere. The second rule adds a new desire to go back to the base if the agent believes that it has a gold nugget.

```
species miner skills: [moving] control:simple_bdi {
    float speed <- 3.0;
    rgb mycolor<-rnd_color(255);
    point target;


    predicate has_gold <- new_predicate("has_gold");
    predicate define_gold_target <- new_predicate("define_gold_target") with_priority 3;
    predicate get_gold <- new_predicate("get_gold") with_priority 2;
    predicate wander <- new_predicate("wander");
    predicate return_base <- new_predicate("return_base") with_priority 4;

}
```

Fig. 7. GAML code of the miner species and variables

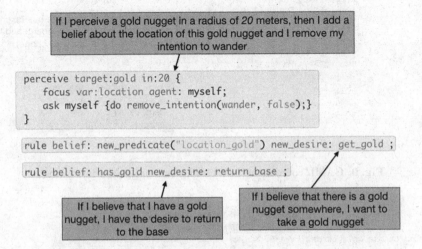

Fig. 8. GAML code for the miner perception and rules

The species uses four plans (Figs. 9 and 10):

- **letsWander:** to achieve the *wander* intention, the agent randomly moves.
- **getGold:** to achieve the *get_gold* intention, the agent moves toward one of the gold nugget that it knows and take it.
- **choose_gold_target:** to achieve the *define_gold_target* intention, the agent chooses its closest known gold nuggets as target.
- **return_to_base:** to achieve the *return_base* intention, the agent returns to its base.

4 Experiments

4.1 Modelers Feedback Analysis

Context of the Experiment. In order to validate our claim that our architecture is simple to use and is adapted to several types of users, we carried out an

```
plan letsWander intention:wander {
    do wander;
}
```

plan aiming at accomplishing the *wander* desire in which the agent randomly moves

```
plan getGold intention:get_gold
{
    if (target = nil) {
        do add_subintention(get_gold,define_gold_target, true);
        do current_intention_on_hold();
    } else {
        do goto target: target ;
        if (target = location)  {
            gold current_gold <- gold first_with (target = each.location);
            if current_gold != nil {
                do add_belief(has_gold);
                ask current_gold {do die;}
            }
            do remove_belief(new_predicate("location_gold",
                    ["location_value"::target]));
            target <- nil;
            do remove_intention(get_gold, true);
        }
    }
}
```

plan aiming at accomplishing the *get_gold* desire

If I have no target, I add a sub-desire to define one

Otherwise, I move toward my target

If I arrived at destination

If the gold nugget exists (i.e. no one has taken it before me), I take it (kill the gold agent) and I add the belief that I have a gold nugget

I remove my belief that their is a gold nugget here and I remove my intention (and desire) to take a gold nugget

Fig. 9. GAML code of the *letsWander* and *get_gold* miner plans

instantaneous plan aiming at accomplishing the *define_gold_target* desire

```
plan choose_gold_target intention: define_gold_target instantaneous: true{
    list<point> possible_golds <- get_beliefs("location_gold") collect
(point(predicate(each).values["location_value"]));
    if (empty(possible_golds)) {
        do remove_intention(get_gold, true);
    } else {
        target <- (possible_golds with_min_of (each distance_to self)).location;
    }
    do remove_intention(define_gold_target, true);
}
```

I build the list of locations where I belief there are gold nuggets.

If I know no location, I remove the intention to take a gold nugget

Otherwise I choose as target the closest gold nugget

I remove the intention (and desire) to define a new target

```
plan return_to_base intention: return_base {
    do goto target: the_base ;
    if (the_base.location = location)  {
        do remove_belief(has_gold);
        do remove_intention(return_base, true);
        the_base.golds <- the_base.golds + 1;
    }
}
```

plan aiming at accomplishing the *return_base* desire

I move toward my base and if I arrive at destination, I remove the belief that I have gold and the intention (and desire) to return to base.

Fig. 10. GAML code of the *choose_gold_target* and *return_to_base* miner plans

experiment with six modelers with different backgrounds: 3 computer scientists, and 3 geographers, all of whom knew GAMA (at least the basic concepts). Two of them have a low level in programming (2 geographers) and four a higher level (1 geographer and 3 computer scientists). All of them have at least a low (2) or medium (3) level in GAMA (they know at least the basic concepts), the last one being an expert. Only the 3 computer scientists know the BDI paradigm.

This experiment consisted in a short lesson (45 min) about the *simpleBDI* architecture, followed by an exercise which required to use this architecture (2 h). At the end of the exercise, each participant answered a short survey to assess the architecture (with both open questions and closed scaled assessments). All these documents (introduction course, exercise, models developed by the different modelers, and their answers to the questionnaire) are available on the project website [1].

The presentation of the *simpleBDI* architecture used a simple gold miner model to present the underlying concepts. The exercise thematic was the evacuation of the city of Rouen (France) (see Fig. 11). A technological hazard is simulated in one of the buildings of the city center. Drivers can perceive the hazard at a distance of 400 m. Those who know that there is a hazard try to reach one of the evacuation sites (shelters). A driver who sees (in a radius of 10 m) another driver trying to evacuate has a small chance to understand that a hazard is happening.

The participants were given a basic GAMA simulation model for that situation, using four species of agents: road, hazard, evacuation site and driver. The behavior of the driver agents is defined by a single reflex executed at each simulation step: the agent moves towards a random target (any point on the road network), and if it reaches its destination, it chooses a new random target. A weighted graph is used for the movement of drivers: they first compute the shortest path between their location and their target, then use this path to move. The weights of the edges of the graph (roads) are updated every 10 simulation steps to take into account the number of drivers on each road. The agent speed on each road is derived from the number of drivers on this road and its maximum capacity. If a driver already has a computed path, it will not recompute it even if the weights of that path change. At the initialization of the model, the roads (154), evacuation sites (7) and the hazard (1) agents are created and initialized using shapefiles; then 500 driver agents are created and randomly situated on the roads. The GAML code for the driver species is given Fig. 12. In this first basic model, drivers do **not** perceive the hazard and do **not** try to reach evacuation sites; they just keep moving randomly.

The exercise was composed of two steps of increasing difficulty:

- **Step 1:** modification of the behaviors of the driver agents, in order to:
  - make them aware of the hazard: via its direct perception (with a probability of 0.2 if they are in a radius of 400 m) or indirectly when they see other driver agents trying to reach an evacuation site (with a probability of 0.01 in a radius of 10 m);
  - make them try to reach the closest shelter (euclidean distance) when they know that there is a hazard.

– **Step 2:** modification of the behaviors of the driver agents and of the evacuation site, so that:
  - if a driver agent trying to reach a shelter thinks that its road is blocked (speed coefficient lower than 0.5), then it should test a new path (recomputation of the path according to the current weights of the graph);
  - drivers take into account the maximum capacity of the evacuation sites (50 drivers each). To know that an evacuation site is full, drivers have to be less than 20 m away from it.

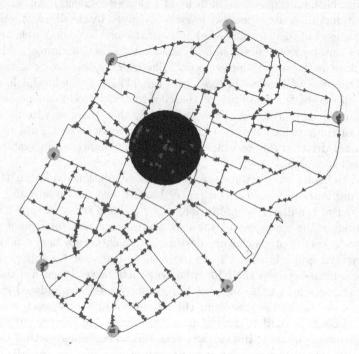

Fig. 11. Snapshot of the city evacuation model: the red circle is the hazard perception area, the green circles the evacuation sites and the blue triangles the drivers. (Color figure online)

Possible Solution of the Exercise. We present here a possible solution. We first add the *simpleBDI* architecture to the driver species and 3 new variables (Fig. 13):

– **escape_mode:** boolean to indicate if the agent is evacuating or not.
– **recompute_path:** boolean to indicate if the agent has to recompute its path or not.
– **current_shelter:** the current evacuation site to reach.

```
species driver skills: [moving]{
    point target;
    float speed <- 30 #km/#h;
    rgb color <- #blue;

    reflex move {
        if (target = nil) {
            target <- any_location_in(one_of(road));
        }
        do goto target: target on: road_network
            move_weights: current_weights recompute_path: false;
        if (location = target) {
            target <- nil;
        }
    }

    aspect default {
        draw triangle(10) rotate: heading + 90 color: color;
    }
}
```

> if I do not have any target, I choose as target a random point in one of the road

> I move toward my target on the road graph

> If I arrived at destination, I set my target to nil

Fig. 12. Initial GAML code for the driver species using reflex architecture, provided to the modelers.

as well as 4 predicates that will be used as the content of mental attitudes:

- **at_target:** the agent is at its target used as the desire to go to a specific target.
- **in_shelter:** the agent is in an evacuation site used as the desire to go to an evacuation site.
- **has_target:** the agent has a defined target used as the desire to define a target.
- **has_shelter:** the agent has selected an evacuation site used as the desire to choose an evacuation site.

```
species driver skills: [moving] control: simple_bdi{
    point target;
    float speed <- 30 #km/#h;
    rgb color <- #blue;
    bool escape_mode <- false;
    predicate at_target <- new_predicate("at_target") with_priority 1;
    predicate in_shelter <- new_predicate("shelter") with_priority 5;
    predicate has_target <- new_predicate("has target") with_priority 2;
    predicate has_shelter <- new_predicate("has shelter") with_priority 10;
    bool recompute_path <- false;
    shelter current_shelter;
}
```

> If true, it means that I am trying to reach an evacuation site

> If true, it means that I will try to recompute my path

> Current evacuation site that I want to reach

Fig. 13. Possible solution GAML code for the driver species and variables.

We define 4 perceptions (Fig. 14):

- **hazard:** perceives the hazard in a radius of 400 m with a probability of 0.2.
- **driver:** perceives the drivers in escape mode in a radius of 10 m with a probability of 0.01.
- **road:** perceives the blocked roads in a radius of 1.
- **shelter:** perceives the full evacuation sites in a radius of 20 m.

```
perceive target:hazard in: 400 when: not escape_mode and flip(0.2){
    focus var: location;
    ask myself {
        do to_escape_mode;
    }
}
```
If I am not in escape mode, I have a probability of 0.2 to perceive a hazard in a distance of 400m. If I perceive a hazard, I add a belief concerning its location and I enter in escape mode

```
perceive target:driver in: 10 when: not escape_mode {
    if (escape_mode and flip(0.01)) {
        focus var:escape_mode;
        ask myself {
            do to_escape_mode;
        }
    }
}
```
If I am not in escape mode, I have a probability of 0.01 to perceive another driver in escape mode in a distance of 10m. If I perceive a hazard, I add a belief concerning the state of the driver and I enter in escape mode

```
perceive target:road where (each.speed_coeff < 0.5) in: 1 when: escape_mode {
    if not (myself.has_belief(new_predicate("name_road", ["name_value"::name]))) {
        myself.recompute_path <- true;
        focus var:name;
    }
}
```
If I am in escape mode and if I perceive a block road in a distance of 1m and I do not have any belief concerning the fact that this road is block, I add this belief and I recompute my path.

```
perceive target:shelter where (each.full) in: 20 when: escape_mode {
    focus var: name;
    myself.current_shelter <- nil;
}
```
If I am in escape mode and if I perceive a full shelter in a distance of 20m I add a belief that this shelter is full and I set my current shelter to nil

Fig. 14. Possible solution GAML code for the driver perceptions

We define two rules to infer the desire to go toward an evacuation site (if the agent perceived the hazard directly or through the observation of escaping drivers) and an action to switch to escape mode (Fig. 15).

Finally, we define four plans for the agents (Figs. 16 and 17):

- **normal_move:** the agent chooses a target if it has none and moves towards it.
- **choose_normal_target:** the agent chooses a random target.
- **evacuation:** the agent chooses an evacuation site if it has none and moves towards it.
- **choose_shelter:** the agent chooses an evacuation site.

If I believe that there is a hazard somewhere, I add the desire to reach an evacuation site

```
rule belief: new_predicate("location_hazard") new_desire: in_shelter;
rule belief: new_predicate("escape_mode_people") new_desire: in_shelter;

action to_escape_mode {
    escape_mode <- true;
    color <- #red;
    target <- nil;
    do remove_intention(at_target, true);
}
```

If I believe that some drivers are trying to reach an evacuation site, I add the desire to reach an evacuation site

If I pass to escape mode, I remove my intention to go somewhere

Fig. 15. Possible solution GAML code for the driver rules and action

```
plan normal_move intention: at_target  {
    if (target = nil) {
        do add_subintention(get_current_intention(),has_target);
        do current_intention_on_hold(at_target);
    } else {
        do goto target: target on: road_network
          move_weights: current_weights recompute_path: false;
        if (target = location)  {
            target <- nil;
        }
    }
}

plan choose_normal_target intention: has_target instantaneous: true{
    target <- any_location_in(one_of(road));
    do remove_intention(has_target, true);
}
```

If I have no shelter, I add a sub-desire to define one

Otherwise, I move toward my target

If I arrive at destination, I set my target to nil

I choose as current target a random point in one of the road

I remove my intention to choose a new target

Fig. 16. Possible solution GAML code for the *normal_move* and *choose_normal_target* driver plans.

Results of the Experiment. After the exercise, each participant answered a short survey about the BDI architecture. The survey was composed of 7 closed questions using a 1–5 scale, 2 yes/no questions and 9 open questions/commentary sections. The first three questions were used to assess the participant background and the others to assess the *simpleBDI* architecture and the exercise performance. Due to the low number of participants, the survey results are used as a qualitative evaluation, and not as a statistically significant quantitative assessment.

A first analysis of the results shows that all the participants find the proposed architecture clear (answer values of 4 or more for that question). Furthermore, the three participants that have a background in BDI architectures find that our architecture translates the BDI paradigm well (3+ answers). Concerning the simplicity of use of the architecture inside GAMA, three of the participants find it good (4) or very good (5), and two pretty good (3).

```
plan evacuation intention: in_shelter  {
    if (current_shelter = nil) {
        do add_subintention(get_current_intention(),has_shelter);
        do current_intention_on_hold(in_shelter);
    }
    else  {
        do goto target: target on: road_network
           move_weights: current_weights recompute_path: recompute_path;
        recompute_path <- false;
        if (target = location and not current_shelter.full){
            do die;
        }
    }
}
```

> If I have no shelter, I add a sub-desire to define one

> Otherwise, I move toward my target

> If I arrive at destination and if the evacuation site is not full, I remove myself from the simulation

```
plan choose_shelter intention: has_shelter instantaneous: true{
    list<shelter> possible_shelters <- (shelter where
        not(self.has_belief(new_predicate("name_shelter",["name_value"::each.name])))));
    current_shelter <- possible_shelters closest_to self;
    target <- current_shelter.location;
    do remove_intention(has_shelter, true);
}
```

> I remove my intention to choose a new shelter

> I choose as current shelter the closest one

> I build the list of possible evacuation sites: the ones that I do not know that they are full

Fig. 17. Possible solution GAML code for the *evacuation* and *choose_shelter* driver plans.

Five out of the six participants succeeded in implementing Step 1, but none of them achieved Step 2. A tentative explanation is that two hours was a too short time to understand what was asked in the exercise, formalize the behavior of the agents using the *simpleBDI* architecture, write the GAML code, and test it. In addition, only one of the participants knew GAMA very well, so as mentioned in the survey, most of the others lost a lot of time searching for specific GAMA operators (not linked with the *simpleBDI* architecture). Nevertheless, four of the participants were very close to succeed in the second step of the exercise (the three computer scientists and one of the geographers).

Concerning the comparison to other architectures, one of the modelers (the BDI expert) preferred *simpleBDI* to the others, while two of them found *simpleBDI* to be complementary to the existing ones, and mentioned that it allows to define the behavior in a simpler way, avoiding to write many complex reflexes. Only one modeler mentioned that they preferred the reflex architecture as they were more used to it. The last two participants did not answer this question.

An interesting remark is that some of the participants mixed the *simpleBDI* and *reflex* architectures, using the BDI architecture to define perceptions and objectives (especially the agents target), and reflexes for the repetitive operational behaviors (moving).

To conclude, this first experiment showed very promising results: all the participants found the *simpleBDI* architecture clear and easy to use. After a short 45 min lesson, they were able to apply it to a real model previously unknown to them. To achieve a more complete and efficient use of the *simpleBDI* architecture, they would however have needed more time, better programming skills in GAMA, and/or a better knowledge of the BDI paradigm.

4.2   Architecture Scalability

In order to test the architecture scalability, we used the two previous models (gold miners and city evacuation) with an increasing numbers of agents.

As GAMA is often used by modelers with old computers (for social simulation in developing countries), we chose to carry out the experiment with a 5-year old Macbook pro (2011) with an i7 processor and 4Go of RAM.

The gold miner model was tested with 10 000 miners, 1000 golds and a square environment of 10×10 km. The simulation was stopped when all the gold nuggets had been returned to the base. The average duration of a simulation step (without any graphical display) was 140 ms.

The evacuation model was tested with 1000 drivers (due to the road network used and how the capacity of roads was defined, it was not possible to test the model with more driver agents - all the road would have been blocked) and a capacity for each of the evacuation sites of 200 driver agents. We stopped the simulation when all the drivers reached an evacuation site. The average duration of a simulation step (with no graphical display) was 70 ms.

The results obtained in terms of performance show that the architecture can already be used with medium-scale real world problems. However, the architecture will still be continuously optimized and we plan to compare the results with other GAMA architectures (especially the reflex one). We also plan in the future to test the architecture with more complex agents having many possible desires, sub-desires and plans.

5   Conclusion

In this paper, we have presented a new BDI architecture dedicated to simulations. This architecture is integrated into the GAMA modeling and simulation platform and directly usable through the GAML language, making it easily usable even by non-computer scientists. We have presented a first experiment that was carried out with modelers with different profiles (geographers and computer scientists). This first experiment showed that our plug-in can be used even by modelers that have little knowledge in programming and Artificial Intelligence, and that it allows to simulate several thousands of agents.

If our architecture is already usable, some improvements are planned. First, we want to improve the inference capabilities of our architecture: when a new belief is added to the belief base, desire and intention bases should be updated in a efficient way as well. Second, we want to make it even more modular by adding more possibilities concerning the choice of plans and desires (beyond just choosing that with the highest priority): user-defined selection, multi-criteria decision process, etc. Finally, we want to add the possibility to use high performance computing (distribute the computation on a grid or cluster) to decrease computation time.

Acknowledgement. This work is part of the ACTEUR (Spatial Cognitive Agents for Urban Dynamics and Risk Studies) research project funded by the French Research Agency (ANR).

References

1. ACTEUR (2015). http://www.acteur-anr.fr
2. GAMA (2015). http://gama-platform.org
3. Adam, C., Gaudou, B.: BDI agents in social simulations: a survey. Knowl. Eng. Rev. **31**, 207–238 (2016)
4. Balke, T., Gilbert, N.: How do agents make decisions? A survey. J. Artif. Soc. Soc. Simul. **17**(4), 31 (2014)
5. Balmer, M., Rieser, M., Meister, K., Charypar, D., Lefebvre, N., Nagel, K., Axhausen, K.: Matsim-t: Architecture and simulation times. In: Multi-Agent Systems for Traffic and Transportation, Engineering, pp. 57–78 (2009)
6. Bellifemine, F., Poggi, A., Rimassa, G.: JADE-A FIPA-compliant agent framework. In: Proceedings of PAAM, London, vol. 99, p. 33 (1999)
7. Bratman, M.: Intentions, Plans, and Practical Reason. Harvard University Press, Cambridge (1987)
8. Caillou, P., Gaudou, B., Grignard, A., Truong, C.Q., Taillandier, P.: A simple-to-Use BDI architecture for agent-based modeling and simulation. In: Jager, W., Verbrugge, R., Flache, A., de Roo, G., Hoogduin, L., Hemelrijk, C. (eds.) Advances in Social Simulation 2015. AISC, vol. 528, pp. 15–28. Springer, Cham (2017). doi:10.1007/978-3-319-47253-9_2
9. Cohen, P.R., Levesque, H.J.: Intention is choice with commitment. Artif. Intell. **42**, 213–261 (1990)
10. Drogoul, A., Amouroux, E., Caillou, P., Gaudou, B., Grignard, A., Marilleau, N., Taillandier, P., Vavasseur, M., Vo, D.-A., Zucker, J.-D.: Gama: multi-level and complex environment for agent-based models and simulations. In: AAMAS, pp. 1361–1362 (2013)
11. Grignard, A., Taillandier, P., Gaudou, B., Vo, D.A., Huynh, N.Q., Drogoul, A.: GAMA 1.6: advancing the art of complex agent-based modeling and simulation. In: Boella, G., Elkind, E., Savarimuthu, B.T.R., Dignum, F., Purvis, M.K. (eds.) PRIMA 2013. LNCS (LNAI), vol. 8291, pp. 117–131. Springer, Heidelberg (2013). doi:10.1007/978-3-642-44927-7_9
12. Howden, N., Rönnquist, R., Hodgson, A., Lucas, A.: JACK intelligent agents-summary of an agent infrastructure. In: 5th AA (2001)
13. Le, V.M., Gaudou, B., Taillandier, P., Vo, D.A.: A new BDI architecture to formalize cognitive agent behaviors into simulations. In: KES-AMSTA, pp. 395–403 (2013)
14. Myers, K.L.: User guide for the procedural reasoning system. SRI International AI Center Technical Report. SRI International, Menlo Park (1997)
15. Pokahr, A., Braubach, L., Lamersdorf, W.: Jadex: a BDI reasoning engine. In: Bordini, R.H., Dastani, M., Dix, J., El Fallah Seghrouchni, A. (eds.) Multi-Agent Programming. Multiagent Systems, Artificial Societies, and Simulated Organizations (International Book Series), vol. 15, pp. 149–174. Springer, Boston (2005). doi:10.1007/0-387-26350-0_6
16. Rönnquist, R.: The goal oriented teams (GORITE) framework. In: Dastani, M., El Fallah Seghrouchni, A., Ricci, A., Winikoff, M. (eds.) ProMAS 2007. LNCS, vol. 4908, pp. 27–41. Springer, Heidelberg (2008). doi:10.1007/978-3-540-79043-3_2

17. Sakellariou, I., Kefalas, P., Stamatopoulou, I.: Enhancing NetLogo to simulate BDI communicating agents. In: Darzentas, J., Vouros, G.A., Vosinakis, S., Arnellos, A. (eds.) SETN 2008. LNCS, vol. 5138, pp. 263–275. Springer, Heidelberg (2008). doi:10.1007/978-3-540-87881-0_24
18. Singh, D., Padgham, L.: OpenSim: a framework for integrating agent-based models and simulation components. In: Frontiers in Artificial Intelligence and Applications, ECAI 2014, vol. 263, pp. 837–842. IOS Press (2014)
19. Taillandier, P., Therond, O., Gaudou, B.: A new BDI agent architecture based on the belief theory. Application to the modelling of cropping plan decision-making. In: iEMSs (2012)
20. Wilensky, U., Evanston, I.: Netlogo. Center for connected learning and computer based modeling. Technical report, Northwestern University (1999)

Defining a Methodology Based on GPU Delegation for Developing MABS Using GPGPU

Emmanuel Hermellin$^{(\boxtimes)}$ and Fabien Michel

LIRMM – CNRS – University of Montpellier, 161 rue Ada, 34095 Montpellier, France
{hermellin,fmichel}@lirmm.fr

Abstract. Multi-Agent Based Simulation (MABS) is used to study complex systems in many research domains. As the number of modeled agents is constantly growing, using General-Purpose Computing on Graphics Units (GPGPU) appears to be very promising as it allows to use the massively parallel architecture of the GPU (Graphics Processing Unit) to do High Performance Computing (HPC). However, this technology relies on a highly specialized architecture, implying a very specific programming approach. So, to benefit from GPU power, a MABS model need to be adapted to the GPU programming paradigm.

Contrary to some recent research works that propose to hide GPU programming to ease the use of GPGPU, we present in this paper a methodology for modeling and implementing MABS using GPU programming. The idea is to be able to consider any kind of MABS rather than addressing a limited number of cases. This methodology defines the iterative process to be followed to transform and adapt a model so that it takes advantage of the GPU power without hiding the underlying technology. We experiment this methodology on two MABS models to test its feasibility and highlight the advantages and limits of this approach.

Keywords: MABS · GPGPU · Methodology · GPU delegation

1 Introduction

Using Multi-Agent Based Simulation (MABS), computing resources requirements often limit the extent to which a model could be experimented [16]. Considering this issue, General-Purpose computing on Graphics Processing Units (GPGPU) is a relevant way of speeding up MABS. Indeed, Graphics Processing Unit (GPU) is an excellent computational platform which is able to perform general-purpose computations [15]. GPGPU relies on using the massively parallel architecture of usual PC graphics cards for accelerating very significantly the performance of programs[1] [4].

Still, implementing MABS using GPGPU is very challenging because GPU programming relies on a highly specialized hardware architecture [1,18]. Because

---

[1] *e.g.* https://developer.nvidia.com/about-cuda.

© Springer International Publishing AG 2017
L.G. Nardin and L. Antunes (Eds.): MABS 2016, LNAI 10399, pp. 24–41, 2017.
DOI: 10.1007/978-3-319-67477-3_2

the SIMD (*Single Instruction, Multiple Data*, also called Stream Processing) parallel computing model on which GPGPU is based consists in executing simultaneously a series of operations on a dataset. An efficient GPU implementation requires that the MABS is modeled by means of distributed and independent data structures. Moreover, usual object oriented features, which are very common in Agent-Based Models (ABM), are no longer available using GPGPU [3].

Among research works that aim at enabling the use of GPGPU in a MABS context, most of them release dedicated tools and frameworks which integrate GPGPU through a transparent use of this technology (*e.g.* [21]). However, doing so, such approaches have to abstract many parts of the MABS models and thus handle only specific cases, while there exists a wide variety of MABS models.

In [8], we have studied the relevance of directly using GPGPU (transform or adapt a model) and promoted the idea that a dedicated methodology would be a valuable contribution to the field. Especially, the purpose of such methodology would be twofold: (1) helping potential users to decide if they could benefit from GPGPU considering their models and (2) describing the modeling and implementation process of MABS models without hiding GPU programming.

From a Software Engineering (SE) perspective, this paper details the methodology extracted from the experiment presented in [8] and the development aspects related to this solution. Then, we test this methodology on two models to highlight the advantages and limits of such an approach. Section 2 presents the evolution of the use of GPGPU in MABS. Section 3 describes the methodology which is proposed in this paper. Section 4 experiments the methodology on two models. Section 5 concludes this paper by listing the advantages and limits of the proposed methodology and outlines planed improvements.

2   Related Works and Motivations

Initially designed for graphics rendering, GPU are now able to perform general-purpose computations. The associated programming paradigm consists in executing simultaneously a series of operations on a dataset. When the data structure is suitable (and only if), the massively parallel architecture of the GPU can provide very high performance gains (up to thousands of times faster) [4]. Empirical results from various experiments in a MABS context show that high simulation speeds can be achieved especially with very large agents populations [6]. However, this excellent speedup comes at the expense of modularity, ease of programmability and reusability [18].

The release of CUDA[2] and OpenCL[3] have simplified GPGPU and greatly contributed to increase the number of MABS using this technology. Flame GPU [21] is a flagship example of the possibilities offered by the rise of specialized GPU programming tools for MABS: It is a ready-to-use solution for creating and simulating MABS using GPGPU.

---

[2] Compute Unified Device Architecture,
   e.g. https://developer.nvidia.com/what-cuda.
[3] Open Computing Language, *e.g.* http://www.khronos.org/opencl.

Nonetheless, the existing frameworks are still difficult to reuse and target only a limited number of MABS use cases. Therefore, most of the new research works still start from scratch and put all their attention on acquiring the best computational gains without considering the accessibility, reusability and modularity aspects.

Moreover, as pointed out in [1], implementing a model using GPGPU does not necessarily imply an increase of performance, notably in the field of MABS where many different and heterogeneous architectures can be conceived. Indeed, achieving an efficient implementation requires to take into account the specific programming model that comes with GPU. Therefore, most of MABS using GPGPU are realized in an ad hoc way and only represent one-off solutions.

Until 2011, the most used approach to implement MABS with GPGPU consisted in executing completely the model on the GPU. Called here all-in-GPU, this approach is useful when the main objective is only to accelerate the simulation. But from a software engineering point of view, it is not adapted because all development efforts are lost. Indeed, all-in-GPU implementations are very specific and therefore cannot be reused in other contexts. This is especially true in the scope of works that address the study of flocking [7], crowd [20], traffic simulations [23] or autonomous navigation [2].

Considering these issues, hybrid approaches have been proposed and represent a very attractive alternative because they consist in sharing the execution of the MABS between the CPU and the GPU. Despite the fact that an all-in-GPU implementation is more efficient than an hybrid one, the latter has two main advantages. Firstly, hybrid approaches enable a step further toward more complex MABS models because one can choose what is executed on the GPU according to the nature of the computations (e.g. [11,12]). Secondly, by removing the programming constraints related to all-in-GPU systems, hybrid approaches are by definition more flexible and open to other technologies [12,13], which in turn brings greater modularity and reusability (e.g. the explicit implementation distinction between the agents and the environment in [13,17]).

So, from this overview, works dealing with GPGPU in MABS can be divided into two categories: (1) works that are only interested in performance gains, and which are hardly reusable and (2) works that take into account aspects related to modularity, genericness, reusability and accessibility. However, works from the later category mostly rely on hiding the use of GPGPU through predefined programming languages or interfaces which are based on specific agent and environment models (e.g. [19]). Even though they represent concrete solutions for easing the use of GPGPU in a MABS context, such approaches cannot take into account the wide variety of MABS which can be conceived because they rely on predefined software structures and conceptual models [8].

Consequently, instead of hiding GPGPU, we here argue on the idea that it would be interesting to provide the MABS community with a methodology that would concretely help to adapt and implement a MABS model using directly GPU programming. This would allow to take into account a larger number of models because such an approach would not rely on a predefined agent model and implementation. This paper presents the methodology on which we are working according to this objective.

3 Defining a GPU Methodology Dedicated to MABS

3.1 The GPU Delegation Principle

The GPU delegation principle [13] is based on the fact that it is very difficult to deport the entire MABS model on graphics cards. Inspired by an Agent-Oriented Software Engineering (AOSE) trend which consists in using the environment as a first class abstraction in MAS [24,25], GPU delegation uses an hybrid approach which divides the execution of the MAS model between the CPU and the GPU. Especially, this principle consists in making a clear separation between the agent behaviors, managed by the CPU, and environmental dynamics, handled by the GPU.

To this end, the design guideline underlying this principle is to identify agent computations which can be transformed into environmental dynamics and thus implemented into GPU modules (called *kernel*, these modules contain the computations executed on the GPU). The GPU delegation principle can be stated as follows: *Any agent perceptions and computations that do not modify the agents' states could be translated to an endogenous dynamic of the environment, and thus considered as a potential GPU environment module.*

3.2 Objectives of the GPU Delegation Methodology

As previously mentioned, using GPGPU in the context of MABS remains difficult mainly because of accessibility and reusability issues. In this context, [10] has proposed an overview of several case studies on using the GPU delegation principle for adapting MABS models to GPU programming. Moreover, the various practical results obtained with this approach are detailed and discussed. Especially, all these experiments [8,9,13] showed that this approach is an original and relevant solution which can be generalized in a methodology.

Furthermore, this methodology is different from other developed solutions because it does not hide the used technology and it puts forward a modular iterative modeling process focusing on the reusability of created tools. In this context, this methodology intends to reach four main objectives:

1. Simplify the use of GPGPU in the context of multi-agent based simulations by describing the modeling and implementation process to follow;
2. Define a generic approach which can be applied on a wide variety of models;
3. Promote the reusability of created tools;
4. Help potential users to decide whether they can benefit from GPGPU according to their models.

3.3   Definition of the GPU Delegation Methodology

All the experiments carried out within the scope of GPU delegation [10] allow to extract a design methodology based on the GPU delegation principle and divided into 5 distinct phases (illustrated in Fig. 1). The first step consists in decomposing all the computations which are presents in the model. The second step consists in identifying, among the above listed computations, those which are compliant with the criteria of the GPU delegation principle. The third step consists in checking if the computations identified as compatible with the GPU delegation principle have already been converted into environmental dynamics and therefore if there is a dedicated GPU module that can be reused. The fourth step verifies the compatibility of selected computations with the GPU architecture. The idea is to choose and apply the GPU delegation principle only on computations that will give the best performance gains once translated into GPU modules. The fifth step consists in concretely implementing the GPU delegation principle on computations that respect all previous constraints. So, the workflow of the methodology can be summarized as follows:

1. Decomposing all the computations;
2. Selecting eligible computations according to the GPU delegation criterion;
3. Reusing GPU modules;
4. Evaluating if computations are compatible with GPU architecture;
5. Implementing the GPU delegation.

Step 1: Decomposing Model's Computations. This phase consists in decomposing all the computations used in the model. Carry out such a decomposition is interesting because a number of computations present in the model are not explicit. Highlighting all the computations that are used by the agents to perform their behaviors, by decomposing them into the most possible primitive, will help to implement GPU delegation and thus increase its efficiency on the considered model. With this approach, we do not work with one large *kernel* containing all the GPU computations but with many small and simple *kernels* which allows to capitalize on the modular and hybrid aspect of the GPU delegation principle.

So, the more the model is decomposed in simple computations, the more GPU delegation could be then successfully applied. This decomposition of actions was also identified as important in [5], where a new division of the actions of agents limits the concurrent access to data what increases the overall performance of the model using GPGPU.

Step 2: Identifying Compatible Computations. The selection of computations is an essential step because it relies on deciding which one respect the criterion of the GPU delegation principle and could benefit from GPGPU. If no part of the model is compliant with the GPU delegation criterion, it is therefore useless to go further because, in such a case, the gains brought by GPGPU

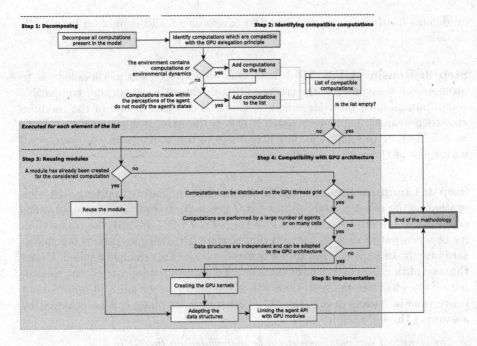

Fig. 1. Diagram of the proposed methodology

could be insignificant or even negative [12]. Moreover, this identification process is different depending on whether the computation is in the environment or in the agent behaviors.

Environment. If the environment is not static and if it contains dynamics, these dynamics must be applied on the entire environment and have a global impact. Indeed, the impact of the dynamics is an important parameter. Take the example of an environmental dynamics which reveals a random amount of food in the environment (at a given position), at each time step of the simulation. This dynamic is well apply to the whole environment but will only have a very localized impact. In this case, translate this dynamic into a GPU module is not justified because the expected gains will be insignificant. Otherwise, if the dynamic has a global impact and respects all specified requirements, the compatibility with the GPU delegation criterion is established and its translation into GPU module is then possible and relevant. The diffusion and the evaporation of digital pheromones [13] is a good example.

Agents. If computations made within the perceptions of the agent do not modify the agents' states, they could be translated into environmental dynamics and then performed by a dedicated GPU module. The idea is to transform a computation realized locally into an environmental dynamic applied in the whole environment. In [13], an agent perception (the computation of pheromone field gradients) has been delegated into the environment and computed by a GPU module.

Step 3: Reusing GPU Modules. One objective of the methodology is to promote the reusability of the created GPU modules. So, given that compatible computations have been identified, it is worth checking if one of the modules created previously could be reused. If this is the case, it is possible to skip to Step 5 in order to adapt the data structures of the computation to correspond with those of the reused module.

Step 4: Computations and GPU Architecture. Before applying GPU delegation on the selected computations, it is necessary to evaluate if computations could fit the massively parallel architecture of the GPU. Indeed, the compatibility of a computation with the criterion of the GPU delegation does not necessarily imply an improvement of performances once this principle applied. Under these conditions, an estimate of the expected gains must be carried out to evaluate if the identified computations will bring performance gains in order to not waste time in useless developments. This assessment phase can be achieved by answering three questions:

- *Do identified computations could be distributed on the GPU ?*
  These computations must be independent and simple and do not contain too many conditional tests which can cause problems or slowing down the execution in GPGPU context (*e.g.* divergence of *threads*, [22]). Computations containing iterative loops are better suited to parallel architectures.
- *Do identified computations are performed in a global way ?*
  Because of the very high data transfer costs between GPU and CPU, if computations are rarely used, triggering a GPU computation could be not efficient even if their are compatible with the principle. So, it is necessary to verify that computations are performed by a large number of agents or applied on a lot of cells (for the environment).
- *Do the data structures associated to the identified computations could fit the GPU architecture ?*
  The data structures used by these computations must be independent from each other and must fit the GPU architecture. Indeed, if the data are not stored by taking into account the constraints of the memory architecture on the GPU, this will impact the overall performance of the model (see [3] for more information on this aspect).

To give an example, based on our different case studies, we recommend in the case of discretized environments the use of arrays or data structures that fit the environment size. So, data will be more suited to the structure of the GPU because, in such case, each cell of the environment will be computed by a *thread*[4].

---

[4] *Thread* is similar to the concept of task: A *thread* may be considered as an instance of the *kernel* which is performed on a restricted portion of the data depending on its location in the global grid of the GPU (its identifier).

Figure 2 illustrates the use of arrays with GPU delegation and Sect. 4.1 describes in details the architecture of a GPU and the associated programming philosophy. With this data structure, agents will only drop off and perceive information (see the example of heatbugs model in Sect. 4.2).

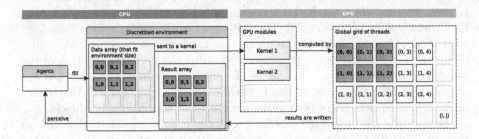

Fig. 2. Structuring data with GPU delegation and a discretized environment

Step 5: Implementation of the GPU Delegation. Implementing GPU delegation can be divided into three parts for each selected computation:

1. Creating the GPU *kernels*;
2. Adapting the data structures;
3. Linking the agent API with the GPU modules.

Applying GPU delegation starts with the creation of the GPU *kernel*, that is the GPU programming version of the selected computation. Thanks to the decomposition which have been done in the identifying step, little GPGPU knowledge is required and the produced *kernels* are easy to implement through a few lines of code (*e.g.* [8]). Then, the data structures need to be adapted to the new GPU module. This adaptation is based on the nature of both the computations and the environment model (arrays fitting the discretization of the environment are mostly used, as recommended previously). Finally, these new elements must be integrated and linked with the CPU part of the model. So, new functions must be created to allow the agents and the environment to collect and use the data computed by the GPU module[5].

4   Experimenting the GPU Delegation Methodology

In this section, we experiment the proposed methodology on two MABS models: *Heatbugs* and *prey/predator*. Specifically, the application of the method on these two models was conducted so as to make explicit the 5 steps of the process in order to define what are the advantages and limitations of such an approach. But first, we present some basics about GPU programming.

---

[5] The TurtleKit platform (http://www.turtlekit.org, [14]) has been used for the development of the GPU delegation principle and methods for the integration of GPGPU were defined only once at the beginning and then reuse for all the next experiments.

4.1 GPGPU Implementation with CUDA

To program on the graphics card and exploit its GPGPU capabilities, we use CUDA which is the GPGPU programming interface provided by Nvidia. The associated programming model relies on the following philosophy[6]: The CPU is called the *host* and plays the role of scheduler. The *host* manages data and triggers *kernels*, which are functions specifically designed to be executed by the GPU, which is called the *device*. The GPU part of the code really differs from sequential code and has to fit the underlying hardware architecture. More precisely, the GPU device is programmed to proceed the parallel execution of the same procedure, the *kernel*, by means of numerous *threads*. These *threads* are organized in *blocks* (the parameters *blockDim.x*, *blockDim.y* characterize the size of these blocks), which are themselves structured in a global grid of blocks.

Each *thread* has unique 3D coordinates (*threadIdx.x*, *threadIdx.y*, *threadIdx.z*) that specifies its location within a *block*. Similarly, each *block* also has three spatial coordinates (respectively *blockIdx.x*, *blockIdx.y*, *blockIdx.z*) that localize it in the global *grid*. So each *thread* works with the same *kernel* but uses different data according to its spatial location within the grid. Moreover, each *block* has a limited *thread* capacity according to the hardware in use. In the remainder of this document, the identifiers of the *threads* in the global grid of the GPU will be denoted by i and j. Figure 3 illustrates this organization for the 2D case. More informations about GPU programming are available in [15,22].

For both of these implementations (heatbugs and prey/predator), the integration of GPU computations was performed in the TurtleKit platform by using the JCUDA library which allows to use CUDA through Java[7].

4.2 The Heatbugs Model

Heatbugs is a model of biologically-inspired agents that attempt to maintain an optimum temperature around themselves. In this model, the bugs (the agents)

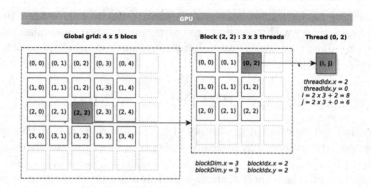

Fig. 3. Thread, blocks, grid organization

---

[6] *e.g.* http://docs.nvidia.com/cuda/.

[7] *e.g.* http://www.jcuda.org.

move around on a 2D environment discretized in cells. A bug may not move to a cell that already has another bug on it. Each bug radiates a small amount of heat which gradually diffuses through the world. Moreover, each bug has an "ideal" temperature it wants to be. The bigger the difference between the cell's temperature and the bug's ideal temperature is high, the more "unhappy" the bug is. When a bug is unhappy (the cell is too cold or too hot), it moves randomly to find a place that better suits those expectations.

Applying the Methodology. The first step consists in enumerating and decomposing all the computations presents in the model (Fig. 4 illustrates this decomposition):

– Environment: Diffusion of the heat emitted by agents (C1).
– Agent: Bugs move (C2), radiate (C3), compute the temperature difference between that of the cell and their ideal temperature (C4) and adjust their happiness (C5).

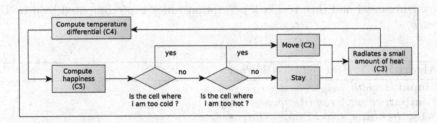

Fig. 4. Summary of behavioral processes of agents in the Heatbugs model

Secondly, we identify eligible computations. The heat diffusion (C1) is an environmental dynamic. So, it is eligible and can be transformed into a GPU *kernel*. C5 consists in perceiving a temperature information and computing the difference between the ideal temperature of the bug and the present temperature according to the value perceived. Because it does not modify the agents' states, it is thus eligible and can be transformed into an environmental dynamics. However, C2, C3 and C4 modify the agents' states, so we do not consider them for the next steps.

Thirdly, we check whether a GPU module exists for the identified computations. C4 has never been implemented in a GPU module in contrary to C1 which consists in computing a diffusion in the environment and was performed several times before [10]. Therefore, we reuse the corresponding GPU module for C1.

Fourthly, we evaluate if these computations can fit the GPU architecture. The heat diffusion is performed for all the cells and data structures used for this computation (a 2D array) are particularly well adapted to the GPU architecture so that GPU delegation could be applied. Considering C4, it can benefit from the GPU power because it consists in computing the difference between two values and can be easily distributed on the whole GPU grid. Moreover, this computation is performed by all the agents at each time step. Finally, we can use 2D arrays for storing the data from this computation.

Fifthly, we implement GPU delegation on the two selected computations. For C1, we use a 2D array (matching the size of the environment) containing the heat value for each cell. It is sent to the GPU that computes simultaneously the heat's diffusion for all the environment. More precisely, for each cell, a sum of heat values from neighboring cells is performed and modulated by a diffusion variable. Algorithm 1 presents the implementation of the corresponding GPU kernel[8].

After the execution of this *kernel*, the heat of each cell is used to compute the *delta* value (C4): The difference between the temperature of the cell where the agent is and the agent's ideal temperature. To this end, agents have previously filled their ideal temperature in a 2D array (fitting the environment size) according to their position. Then, once this computation is done, the agents recover the resulting value (the delta value) in the array and adjust their behavior accordingly. Algorithm 2 presents an implementation of this GPU *kernel*. So, instead of a computation performed in their behavior, the agents now drop information in the environment and then realize a perception which is precomputed by a GPU *kernel*.

Algorithm 1. Heat diffusion *Kernel*

---

    input : $width, height, heatArray, radius$
    output: $resultArray$ (the quantity of heat)
1 $i = blockIdx.x * blockDim.x + threadIdx.x$;
2 $j = blockIdx.y * blockDim.y + threadIdx.y$;
3 $sumOfHeat = 0$;
4 **if** $i < width$ and $j < height$ **then**
5 | $sumOfHeat = \mathrm{getNeighborsHeat}(heatArray[i,j], radius)$;
6 **end**
7 $resultArray[i,j] = sumOfHeat * heatAdjustment$;

To evaluate the model's performance after the application of the methodology, we compare the CPU and hybrid versions[9]. The model is simulated for different environment sizes and a fixed density of agents (40%). Figure 5 presents the acceleration coefficients obtained between the two versions of the model. From this results, we notice that the acceleration coefficient obtained for the environment is more important when the environment is large (*e.g.* the gain reaches x7.5

---

[8] i and j are the coordinates of a *thread* which is considered as an instance of the *kernel*. Each *thread* is performed on a restricted portion of the data depending on its location (these coordinates) in the global GPU architecture grid.

[9] For those tests, the configuration is composed of an Intel i7-4770 processor (Haswell generation, 3.40 GHz) and an Nvidia K4000 graphics card (Kepler architecture, 768 CUDA cores).

Algorithm 2. Delta computation *kernel*

---

   input : *width, height, heatArray, idealTemperatureArray*
   output: *resultArray* (the delta value)
1 $i = blockIdx.x * blockDim.x + threadIdx.x$;
2 $j = blockIdx.x * blockDim.y + threadIdx.y$;
3 *happiness* $= 0$;
4 **if** $i < width$ *and* $j < height$ **then**
5 | *happiness* $= heatArray[i,j] - idealTemperatureArray[i,j]$;
6 **end**
7 *resultArray*$[i,j] = happiness$;

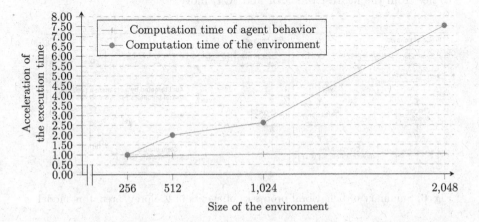

Fig. 5. Performance gains between CPU and hybrid versions of the heatbugs model

for the largest environment). However, the gain for the agents' behavior is low (about 5%). We can explain these results as follows: Environmental dynamics is applied to all the cells and performed by a GPU *kernel* while only a small part of computation made within the agent behavior (the computation of the delta value) has been delegated to a GPU module. Moreover, for the latter, the gain highly depends on the density of agents: If it is too low, the gain may be negative.

4.3 The Prey/Predator Model

The prey/predator model describes the dynamics of biological systems in which two species interact, one as a predator and the other as prey. In our model, the agents evolve in a 2D environment discretized in cells. Predators and prey are placed randomly in the environment. All predators have a *Field Of Vision* (FOV) that reaches 10 cells around them. Predators search for a prey in their FOV. If no prey can be targeted, they move randomly. In the other case, they head to the targeted prey. Prey have a smaller FOV. They randomly move in the environment and when a predator is in their field of vision, they run away in the opposite direction. A prey dies when it is targeted and when one predator is on the same cell.

Applying the Methodology. The first step consists in enumerating and decomposing all the computations present in the model (Fig. 6 illustrates this decomposition):

– The environment is static and does not have any endogenous dynamics.
– Agents: Predators (C1) compute the intercept heading toward the targeted prey and (C2) move, prey (C3) compute the escape heading that allows them to flee from the nearest predator and (C4) move.

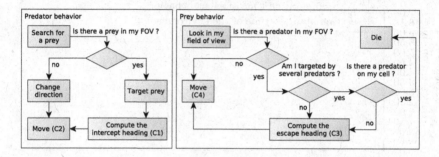

Fig. 6. Summary of behavioral processes of agents in the prey/predators model

Secondly, we identify eligible computations. Among these four computations, C2 and C4 modify the agents' states (the agent's position) while C1 and C3 consist in computing displacement directions that do not modifying the agents' states. So, C1 and C3 can be transformed into environmental dynamics. These dynamics will compute for each cell of the environment the direction toward the closest agent (prey and predator). The agents will only perceive, according to their type, the direction that interest them and act accordingly.

Thirdly, we check whether a GPU module exists for the identified computations. For C1 and C3, we can reuse the *GPU field perception* module previously created in [13] which computes a pheromone field gradients. Indeed, this module computes for each cell of the environment the direction of neighboring cells with the greatest/smallest amount of a given data. Here, the data is the presence or absence of agents in the neighborhood.

Fourthly, we evaluate if these computations can fit the GPU architecture. Given that we reuse an existing module, and no new computation has been identified as compatible, we can directly go to step 5 because we know that C1 and C3 can fit the GPU architecture.

Fifthly, we implement GPU delegation on the two selected computations. For C1 and C3, we reuse one *kernel* already created in previous works. It will just be necessary to adapt the data that will be sent to this *kernel*. C1 and C3 being similar computations, we only take as an example the implementation of C3.

Algorithm 3. The presence gradient *kernel*

---

   input : *width, height, preyMark*[]
   output: *preyMaxDirection*[]
1 *i = blockIdx.x * blockDim.x + threadIdx.x* ;
2 *j = blockIdx.y * blockDim.y + threadIdx.y* ;
3 *float max = 0* ;
4 *int maxIndex = 0* ;
5 **if** *i < width* **and** *j < height* **then**
6   **for** *int u = 1 ; u < 8; u + +* **do**
7   *float current* = getNeighborsValues(*u, preyMark*[*i, j*]);
8   **if** *max < current* **then**
9   *max = current*;
10   *maxIndex = u*;
11   **end**
12   **end**
13   *preyMaxDirection*[*i, j*] = *maxIndex * 45* ;
14 **end**

So, each prey sets down a presence mark in a two-dimensional array (`preyMark`) according to its location. The presence mark is all the greater as there are prey in the neighborhood. Then, this array is sent to the GPU module which tests the vicinity of each cell of the environment and determines the direction leading to the strongest presence mark. The directions are written in a second array (`preyMaxDirection`). Predators only have to perceive in this array the heading value leading to the nearest prey. Algorithm 3 presents an implementation of this GPU *kernel*.

It is the same process for C1: Each predators sets down a presence mark in a two-dimensional array (`predatorsMark`) which is sent to the GPU module. Prey only perceive in the result array (`predatorsMaxDirection`) the heading value leading to the nearest predators and flee according to this value.

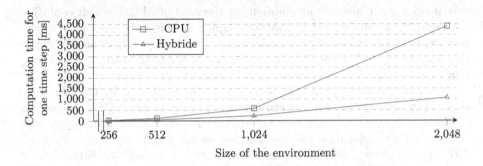

Fig. 7. Performance between CPU and hybrid versions of the prey/predator model.

To evaluate model's performance after the application of the methodology, we compare the CPU and hybrid versions[10]. The model is simulated for different environment sizes and a fixed density of agents (40%). The distribution between prey and predators is the following: 90% of prey and 10% of predators. Figure 7 presents the computation time for one time step obtained for the two versions of the model.

From this results, we notice that the performance difference between the two versions of the model increase with the size of the environment. This observation has already been made in our previous work [10].

5   Conclusion and Future Work

This paper presented a methodology for modeling and implementing MABS using GPU programming, namely GPU delegation. It is based on [9,13] and extracted from the experiment conducted in [8,10]. The long term goal of the GPU delegation methodology is to provide a complete workflow for actually considering GPU programming in the context of MABS, that is (1) without hiding this technology to the user and (2) by promoting an iterative modeling process that put forward software engineering aspects such as modularity and reusability.

Compared to existing works which are related to the use of GPU programming in MABS, one main advantage of the proposed methodology is accessibility. Indeed, considering the two experiments presented in this paper, we have seen that applying the GPU delegation methodology workflow is easy and helps to identify which parts of a MABS model could be considered for GPU programming. Especially, we have seen that it was possible to find eligible computations on the two selected models. Moreover, we have seen that this workflow promotes modularity and thus reusability, which is an advantage of this approach compared to other existing works. For instance, considering the heatbugs model, we have been able to directly reuse a *kernel* (for the heat diffusion) which has been achieved in another context (for [8]).

Another advantage of GPU delegation relies on its versatility in the sense that it does not make any assumption on the kind of MABS which could be envisaged. Especially, considering all the adapted models and experiments which have led to the definition of this methodology (*e.g.* [8,9,13]), one can see that a wide variety of use cases have been implemented: Reynolds boids, game of life, Schelling's segregation, fire spreading, heatbugs, prey/predator, etc.

As a first limitation, this last point has to be moderated by the fact that most of our use cases embed discretized environments for which GPU delegation is relatively easy to achieve in terms of implementation. So, one future work will be to test GPU delegation of more heterogeneous models and use cases (*e.g.* with continuous environments), strengthening its scope of applicability.

Another limit is about its ability to be used for deciding if a particular model is worth porting on the GPU or not. Indeed, as we have seen in this paper, even

---

[10] For those tests, we reuse the same configuration as previously detailed.

if a model validates the second step (containing eligible computations), in some cases, the performance gains could be low. This is particularly true when the model does not contain environmental dynamics. In such a case, obtaining performance gains only depends on the number of agents which is simulated. If this number is small, the gain could be insignificant or even negative (*e.g.* as for the heatbugs model). In fact, we are here facing one limit of the proposed methodology in the sense that we cannot predict in advance the benefits of the application of the methodology. In such a case, the application of the methodology is very dependent on the parameters of the model and on the hardware configuration. So, determining the threshold above which GPU delegation could be useful still requires an empirical evaluation.

For addressing this last issue, one research perspective is to develop a software solution (benchmark), that one could run on his particular hardware configuration to have an idea of the threshold above which a GPU implementation could be worth doing. More specifically, the idea is to develop a set of common agent computation patterns (GPU *kernels*) which would be used to test the relevance of applying GPU delegation considering both the hardware platform and the MABS model.

References

1. Aaby, B.G., Perumalla, K.S., Seal, S.K.: Efficient simulation of agent-based models on multi-GPU and multi-core clusters. In: Proceedings of the 3rd International ICST Conference on Simulation Tools and Techniques, SIMUTools 2010, pp. 29:1–29:10. ICST (Institute for Computer Sciences, Social-Informatics and Telecommunications Engineering), Brussels (2010)
2. Bleiweiss, A.: Multi agent navigation on the GPU. In: Games Developpement Conference (2009)
3. Bourgoin, M., Chailloux, E., Lamotte, J.-L.: Efficient abstractions for GPGPU programming. Int. J. Parallel Program. **42**(4), 583–600 (2014)
4. Che, S., Boyer, M., Meng, J., Tarjan, D., Sheaffer, J.W., Skadron, K.: A performance study of general-purpose applications on graphics processors using CUDA. J. Parallel Distrib. Comput. **68**(10), 1370–1380 (2008)
5. Coakley, S., Richmond, P., Gheorghe, M., Chin, S., Worth, D., Holcombe, M., Greenough, C.: Large-scale simulations with FLAME. In: Intelligent Agents in Data-intensive Computing, pp. 123–142. Springer International Publishing, Cham (2016)
6. D'Souza, R.M., Lysenko, M., Rahmani, K.: SugarScape on steroids: simulating over a million agents at interactive rates. In: Proceedings of Agent 2007 Conference (2007)
7. Erra, U., Frola, B., Scarano, V., Couzin, I.: An efficient GPU implementation for large scale individual-based simulation of collective behavior. In: International Workshop on High Performance Computational Systems Biology, HIBI 2009, pp. 51–58, October 2009
8. Hermellin, E., Michel, F.: GPU delegation: toward a generic approach for developping MABS using GPU programming. In: The Proceedings of the International Conference on Autonomous Agents and Multiagent Systems, AAMAS, Singapore, pp. 1249–1258 (2016)

9. Hermellin, E., Michel, F.: GPU environmental delegation of agent perceptions: application to Reynolds's boids. In: Gaudou, B., Sichman, J.S. (eds.) MABS 2015. LNCS, vol. 9568, pp. 71–86. Springer, Cham (2016). doi:10.1007/978-3-319-31447-1_5

10. Hermellin, E., Michel, F.: Overview of case studies on adapting MABS models to GPU programming. In: Bajo, J., Escalona, M.J., Giroux, S., Hoffa-Dąbrowska, P., Julián, V., Novais, P., Sánchez-Pi, N., Unland, R., Azambuja-Silveira, R. (eds.) PAAMS 2016. CCIS, vol. 616, pp. 125–136. Springer, Cham (2016). doi:10.1007/978-3-319-39387-2_11

11. Laville, G., Mazouzi, K., Lang, C., Marilleau, N., Herrmann, B., Philippe, L.: MCMAS: a toolkit to benefit from many-core architecure in agent-based simulation. In: an Mey, D., et al. (eds.) Euro-Par 2013. LNCS, vol. 8374, pp. 544–554. Springer, Heidelberg (2014). doi:10.1007/978-3-642-54420-0_53

12. Laville, G., Mazouzi, K., Lang, C., Marilleau, N., Philippe, L.: Using GPU for multi-agent multi-scale simulations. In: Omatu, S., De Paz Santana, J., González, S., Molina, J., Bernardos, A., Rodríguez, J. (eds.) Distributed Computing and Artificial Intelligence. Advances in Intelligent and Soft Computing, vol. 151, pp. 197–204. Springer, Heidelberg (2012)

13. Michel, F.: Translating agent perception computations into environmental processes in multi-agent-based simulations: a means for integrating graphics processing unit programming within usual agent-based simulation platforms. Syst. Res. Behav. Sci. 30(6), 703–715 (2013)

14. Michel, F., Beurier, G., Ferber, J.: The turtlekit simulation platform: application to complex systems. In: Akono, A., Tonyé, E., Dipanda, A., Yétongnon, K. (eds.) Workshops Sessions of the Proceedings of the 1st International Conference on Signal-Image Technology and Internet-Based Systems, SITIS 2005, Yaoundé, Cameroon, pp. 122–128. IEEE, 27 November–1 December 2005

15. Owens, J.D., Luebke, D., Govindaraju, N., Harris, M., Krüger, J., Lefohn, A.E., Purcell, T.J.: A survey of general-purpose computation on graphics hardware. Comput. Graph. Forum 26(1), 80–113 (2007)

16. Parry, H., Bithell, M.: Large scale agent-based modelling: a review and guidelines for model scaling. In: Heppenstall, A.J., Crooks, A.T., See, L.M., Batty, M. (eds.) Agent-Based Models of Geographical Systems, pp. 271–308. Springer, Netherlands (2012)

17. Pavlov, R., Müller, J.: Multi-agent systems meet GPU: deploying agent-based architectures on graphics processors. In: Camarinha-Matos, L., Tomic, S., Graça, P. (eds.) Technological Innovation for the Internet of Things. IFIP Advances in Information and Communication Technology, vol. 394, pp. 115–122. Springer, Heidelberg (2013)

18. Perumalla, K.S., Aaby, B.G.: Data parallel execution challenges and runtime performance of agent simulations on GPUs. In: Proceedings of the 2008 Spring Simulation Multiconference, pp. 116–123 (2008)

19. Richmond, P., Coakley, S., Romano, D.M.: A high performance agent based modelling framework on graphics card hardware with CUDA. In: Proceedings of The 8th International Conference on Autonomous Agents and Multiagent Systems - vol. 2, Volume 2 of AAMAS 2009, pp. 1125–1126. International Foundation for Autonomous Agents and Multiagent Systems, Richland (2009)

20. Richmond, P., Romano, D.M.: A high performance framework for agent based pedestrian dynamics on GPU hardware. In: European Simulation and Modelling (2011)

21. Richmond, P., Walker, D., Coakley, S., Romano, D.M.: High performance cellular level agent-based simulation with FLAME for the GPU. Brief. Bioinform. **11**(3), 334–347 (2010)
22. Sanders, J., Kandrot, E.: CUDA by Example: An Introduction to General-Purpose GPU Programming. Pearson, Boston (2011)
23. Strippgen, D., Nagel, K.: Multi-agent traffic simulation with CUDA. In: International Conference on High Performance Computing Simulation, HPCS 2009, pp. 106–114, June 2009
24. Weyns, D., Van Dyke Parunak, H., Michel, F., Holvoet, T., Ferber, J.: Environments for multiagent systems state-of-the-art and research challenges. In: Weyns, D., Van Dyke Parunak, H., Michel, F. (eds.) E4MAS 2004. LNCS, vol. 3374, pp. 1–47. Springer, Heidelberg (2005). doi:10.1007/978-3-540-32259-7_1
25. Weyns, D., Michel, F.: In: Weyns, D., Michel, F. (eds.) E4MAS 2014. LNCS (LNAI), vol. 9068. Springer, Cham (2015)

Creating Reproducible Agent Based Models Using Formal Methods

Joseph Kehoe[✉]

Dublin City University, Glasnevin, Dublin 9, Ireland
joseph.kehoe@itcarlow.ie

Abstract. Reproducibility is a problem in Agent Based Modelling. It has proven difficult to replicate results obtained by other researchers so as to confirm their findings. A number of different solutions have been proposed to overcome this issue but the effectiveness of these approaches is still open to debate. Here we propose that formal methods, an approach developed by computer scientists for the production of high integrity systems, can be used to specify even complex Agent Based Models. In order to demonstrate the applicability of Formal Methods we specify Sugarscape, a well known Agent Based Social Simulation, using the Z Notation. Our specification uncovers many ambiguities in the original definition of Sugarscape thus demonstrating the effectiveness of this approach and providing a reference specification of Sugarscape for researchers to use.

1 Introduction

Although Agent Based Modelling (ABM) is becoming more popular across many disciplines there remain questions about its applicability [33]. One of the main issues is that of replication (or reproduction) of results. It is proving difficult for researchers to reproduce the results claimed by other researchers. This is known as the *replication problem*. Efforts are currently underway to tackle this issue by improving ABM specifications.

In Computer Science there is a similar problem, that of writing specifications precise enough to allow system developers to produce an implementation that they can be confident matches the specification. The most precise approach is based in mathematics and termed Formal Methods. A formal specification can be proven to have (or not have) certain (un)desirable properties. It is also possible to mathematically verify or prove that an implementation matches a specification. Formal methods have found a niche in high integrity software development where errors cannot be tolerated (due to, for example, the risk of loss of life).

We propose using formal methods as a way of writing reproducible ABM specifications. To this end we formally specified Sugarscape, a well known and large Agent Based Social Simulation (ABSS[1]), using the Z notation to see if this revealed any inconsistencies in the its original definition.

---

[1] We will use the terms ABM and ABSS interchangeably in this paper.

© Springer International Publishing AG 2017
L.G. Nardin and L. Antunes (Eds.): MABS 2016, LNAI 10399, pp. 42–70, 2017.
DOI: 10.1007/978-3-319-67477-3_3

We found a number of ambiguities in the rule definitions and also discovered a range of missing information leading to incomplete rule definition. We have placed the entire specification online where each rule is formal specified and discussed in detail [27]. We have also used this specification to implement our own version of Sugarscape to test out different updating techniques and benchmark algorithm performance [28]. Here we give an overview of the process of formally specifying Sugarscape and provide conclusions on the suitability of this approach.

1.1 Outline of Paper

We start with a reminder of what the replication problem in ABM is. After this we survey the approaches currently proposed to help overcome this issue. Following on from this we give a brief overview of formal specification in general and Z in particular. Then we give a summary of the Agent Based Social Simulation we have specified, *Sugarscape*. We then demonstrate the efficacy of using formal methods to specify ABSS by listing the issues that the formal specification uncovered. We follow this section with a discussion of the merits of formally specifying ABMs and the possible weaknesses with this approach. The next section summarises our implementation of Sugarscape based on the formal specification. Finally we give our conclusions on the efficacy of this approach.

2 The Replication Problem

The replication problem is simply stated: although simulations are developed in quantity and their results peer reviewed and published it has proven difficult for researchers to replicate these results [11, 20, 36].

Given the nature of ABM, where behaviour is defined in terms of simple agent interactions it might appear, at first glance, that reproducing an ABM defined by another researcher would be easy. However, in reality it has proven very difficult due to a number of factors, for example:

1. The simulation source code is not publicly available;
2. The rules of the model are not defined sufficiently precisely;
3. The updating method (synchronous or asynchronous) is not declared or clearly explained.

If we wish to check that the published results are accurate we must re-implement the simulation ourselves, seldom an easy task. Even then, if our results do not match the original we cannot be sure that it is our implementation that is correct. Modellers need to provide a clear and precise description of the model to work from and this is not always present. There have been a number of attempts to overcome these problems but none have been completely successful.

If the published results of a simulation cannot be replicated then we can have little trust in these results. Being able to repeat or reproduce scientific results is an essential part of science. This can be a particular issue for modellers in the natural sciences who may not be as familiar enough with the computer science required to ensure that their implementation is a correct interpretation of the model.

We posit a new approach, that of using formal methods. Although developed for proving correctness in safety critical systems we will demonstrate that they can be used to tackle the replication problem in ABM.

3   Related Work

3.1   Overview, Design Concepts, and Details

Overview, Design concepts and Details (ODD) [17] is a protocol for specifying Individual Based Models (IBM) and/or ABM. ODD was introduced to overcome shortcomings in published IBM definitions, specifically the issue that IBM are not specified precisely enough to allow for replication of the simulations.

The ODD protocol consists of three blocks (Overview, Design concepts and Details) divided into seven sections:

1. Purpose;
2. State variables and Scales;
3. Process overview and scheduling;
4. Design Concepts;
5. Initialisation;
6. Inputs;
7. Submodels.

By enforcing a particular structure on simulation descriptions it (i) makes specifications easier to read and (ii) ensures that modellers do not forget to specify any aspect of the model. ODD was originally tested by 28 modellers within the field of ecology to test its usefulness. Since its introduction it has been used in over 50 publications [18]. The long term aims of ODD are stated as:

"modellers could describe their IBM on paper using some kind of language that (1) people can understand intuitively, (2) is widely used throughout ecology, (3) provides 'shorthand' conventions that minimize the effort to describe the IBM rigorously and completely, and (4) can be converted directly into an executable simulator without the possibility of programming errors."

These aims seem quite naive from a computer science perspective where similar goals have been attempted for many years without success [5].

ODD has been criticised for not being formal enough [14] and the chasm between the current approach to specifications taken in IBM and those more formal models used in computer science is clear. For example it is stated that it is often the case that the specifications produced by each role in the simulation development process (four are identified: *Thematician, Modeller, Computer Scientist* and *Programmer*) might *stay in the realm of mental models, and never reach materialisation*!

ODD has been extended by adding an algorithmic model to specify the behaviours in the IBM [19]. Although interesting, it is lacking any of the modularisation features used by computing specification languages such as Z [39].

3.2 Model Alignment

An early paper to point out and address this problem [11] concluded that we cannot trust simulation results that have not been replicated. Simulations should be treated like experiments in this regard. They illustrate this by taking a published simulation model and producing two independent implementations of it. They then compared the results of their two independent implementations against the original to find differences in the outcomes. They state that producing two different implementations gave them confidence in their results, where they differed with the original results, that they would not have had with only one implementation.

The process of re-implementing a model they called *model alignment* and they suggest that, as most simulations are not amenable to formal analysis, experimentation is the only route to verification.

While we agree that experimentation is useful it does not solve the problem of specifications that are vague or are missing important information. If we do not agree the rules of the ABM with which we are experimenting it will not help.

3.3 A Model Driven Approach

Following from the conclusion of [11] that experimentation is the only route to verification, [36] list two closely related approaches:

Re-implementation. The model is rewritten following the original authors instructions;

Alignment or Docking. We implement a conceptually identical model *but* using different tools and different methodologies.

They favour alignment as the better approach and propose using an independent modelling process that can be automatically implemented using a number of different ABM toolkits. This has the advantages that it becomes easier for modellers to provide multiple implementations and does not require in depth programming skills from them.

Such an approach would be useful in that a number of implementations can be compared but it still only gives replication, not reproducibility. We can replicate (copy) their results but it does not allow us to reproduce their results. In other words if there is some error in their approach then *Alignment* will not find that error, only repeat it.

3.4 Executable Papers

Hinsen [20–22] identified the problem as belonging to the entire computational science field. His proposed solution is to produce *executable papers*, termed

ActivePapers. That is, published papers will, as well as containing the usual text, also contain the full simulation model, executable code, source code, etc. all in the correct formats in a single HDF[2] format. Then from this executable paper one could extract all the necessary information required to replicate the simulation.

While he recognises and accepts the difference between replicability and reproducibility in science he states that the current state of affairs is unsatisfactory and a symptom of a lack of exchange between the natural sciences and computer science.

3.5 Data Sharing

A similar proposal to *ActivePapers* (above) is made by [30] for embedding data with existing formats (pdf, etc.). Here the suggestion is that no new formats are required and what is missing is only the toolset to allow easy insertion of different data attachments to existing formats. The authors have developed some tools to this end.

All these approaches are useful and give more information to experimenters but all have the same weakness. They only allow us to repeat an experiment exactly as it was done originally. Therefore such approaches do not deal with errors that are hidden in the original experiment. For example, if the updating approach used is the source of the problem then simply copying this approach will give us the same erroneous results.

What is needed is a higher level approach to replication that allows us the freedom to interrogate the original ABM and reproduce the model independently in a verifiable manner.

4 Formal Methods

4.1 Overview

Computer scientists have been trying to solve a problem analogous to replication. The problem is how to be sure that the software being produced matches the specification of the client. We can have confidence in this only if the problem is specified in a precise and unambiguous manner. It has become clear that specifying a problem in a natural language[3] is inappropriate. Natural languages are neither precise nor unambiguous. To overcome these limitations computer scientists sought to base their specifications in mathematics. The process of producing mathematically based specifications is known as formal methods [4,41].

Formal methods are based on strong mathematical foundations usually involving one or more of Logical Calculus, Set and Type theory, Formal Languages, Automata Theory and Program Semantics. The two more popular

---

[2] http://www.hdfgroup.org/.
[3] e.g. English, Mandarin, German, etc.

mathematical approaches are model based, e.g. VDM [26], and process based, e.g. CSP [1].

These approaches place the emphasis on correctness and give benefits such as precision of the system specification and provability of the correctness of the specification and/or implementation. Their main benefit may rest in the discipline they impose on their users, forcing them to explicitly define and think carefully about every part of the system being specified. There are three phases to formally specifying a system, each of which is more difficult than the last:

Specification. Precisely define the system in the underlying mathematical formalism;

Refinement. Mathematically refine the specification from a high level specification to implementation;

Verification. Use the methods proof rules to prove that the implementation correctly interprets the specification and has all the properties we expect (e.g. the safety property[4]).

The most common approach is known as *Formal Methods-lite* where we only proceed with the first step, *Specification.* This still brings many of the benefits of formal specification without the higher overheads (in terms of extra time and mathematical knowledge required) associated with the other two phases. We believe that formal methods-lite is sufficient to solve the replication problem.

4.2   The Z Notation

We chose the Z notation [39] as our specification language. The Z notation is a formal specification language for describing and modelling computer systems. It was first proposed in 1977 by Jean-Raymond Abrial and gained ISO standard accreditation in 2002. It is based on axiomatic set theory, lambda calculus and first order predicate logic. All expressions in Z are typed.

Specification in Z is state-based, that is it is based on a system of states with operations defined in terms of before and after states and the relationship between them. A specification is defined as a series of sequential steps with each step considered to be discrete in nature. This makes Z a good fit for ABMs where simulations are defined as a sequence of atomic steps.

A high level Z specification will be independent of implementation issues and although it is possible to formally refine a Z specification down into computer code this is not necessary. The high level specification only states the before and after states of each operation and any implementation that satisfies these constraints is allowable.

Because Z has been around so long it has evolved into a mature and standardised system that is widely understood within the Formal Methods community. It has a range of software based tools [13] readily available for specifiers that aid with the production of specifications and proving properties of those specifications.

---

[4] Safety properties informally require that "something bad will never happen".

This availability of tools combined with the widespread recognition and maturity of Z alongside its state-based approach makes it a good choice for specifying ABMs. In particular, we have found that the specification of rules in a manner that is completely agnostic as to the implementation approach is a boon. Specifically it allowed us to place no restrictions on what forms of conflict resolution rules are used. It only states the *before* and *after* state of the simulation on application of each rule, not the particular strategy used to get from the before state to the after state.

5 Sugarscape

Sugarscape [12] is the simulation that demonstrated how ABM could be applied to the social sciences. It remains influential today and almost every major simulation toolkit (Swarm, Repast, Mason and NetLogo) [2,24,34] comes with a partial implementation of Sugarscape that demonstrates that toolkit's approach to simulation.

Currently, social science simulations are starting to embrace concurrency in an effort to allow for bigger, more complete and faster implementations of ABMs. Different concurrency researchers [10,31] have used partial implementations of the Sugarscape model as a testbed for benchmarking different approaches to parallelising ABMs. However although the rules of Sugarscape have been defined in [12] there is no general agreement on their exact meaning [3,15]. These difficulties hamper the ability of researchers to properly compare their approaches, provide complete implementations of Sugarscape or replicate the results of other researchers.

It is worth noting that each of the thirteen rules of Sugarscape can be defined in a paragraph of text and appear at first glance to be simple. This shows how deceptive natural language based specifications are, they appear clear but when different researchers try to implement them cannot agree on their exact meaning.

Originally the rules were stated with an explicit assumption that the underlying implementation would be sequential. Concurrency was simulated through randomisation of the order of each rule application on the individual agents. Models that follow this regime are termed *asynchronous*.

Most of the rules require some form of conflict resolution. We have specified the rules in a manner consistent with the original intention (agents acting concurrently) but independent of any particular approach to how this concurrency is implemented. That is, we have refrained from imposing any specific conflict resolution rules or a specific updating approach.

By formalising the simulation and providing a single precisely defined reference for the rules we can produce a standard definition of Sugarscape. Compliance with this single reference allows proper comparisons to be made between different approaches. It also leaves it open to the implementer to decide what approach to conflict resolution they wish to take. We detected ambiguities present in the current rule definitions, provided precise interpretations, where possible, and flagged unresolvable problems where not.

6   Results of the Specification

We produced a formal specification of sugarscape in Z and made this publicly available [27]. This specification covers the entire Sugarscape definition with all 13 rules and two resource types (sugar and spice).

We made the decision to restrict the initial specification to one pollution type and one resource type in an effort to guarantee clarity. While the original rules were designed so that they could be extended to arbitrary numbers of resources and pollutants, explicitly specifying an arbitrary number of resources and pollutants would make the specification more difficult to understand and thus more likely to either contain or cause mistakes. This specification extends to about 46 pages in length including embedded explanatory text.

Once we produced a specification for the single resource scenario we extended the specification to a two resource situation (where the two resources are known as *sugar* and *spice*). This allowed us to specify the final rule, *Trade*, as that rule requires two resources to function.

This allowed for:

1. A simpler and easier to understand specification of the rules that use only one resource (trading clarity against completeness);
2. A complete (but separate) specification for simulations that use two resources.

The downside of this is that each rule has to be specified twice, once for the single resource scenario and once for the two resource scenario. Fortunately a modeller will only need to read one version of the rule depending on the number of resources in the simulation. We do not provide specifications for multiple pollutants as multiple pollutants were never actually implemented in Sugarscape. While specifying multiple pollutants would make for a more general specification there is a trade off in terms of the complexity this would add. If the specification becomes too complex it can make it more difficult to reason about. As multiple pollutants are never used we do not feel this is too much of a limitation.

Similarly we did not provide a specification for more than two resources as we deem the benefits of doing so counterbalanced by both the complexity of the resulting specification and the lack of any requirement to use such a complex simulation for benchmarking purposes. Sugarscape has only ever been implemented with two resource types. Anyone wishing to extend Sugarscape further can use the two resource specification for guidance.

6.1   The Specification Process

A Z specification will generally be broken down into the following steps. First we define any necessary constants. Alongside these constants we define new types, outside of the built-in types provided by Z, that are required for the specification. After this we specify the state of the system being specified. This state definition will include all the information held by the system alongside any *invariants* or properties that hold for the lifetime of the system. Once the state has been defined we define the initial state of the system which assigns the appropriate initial values that the system will have on startup. With all this in place the operations that can occur within the system are individually defined. Each operation is defined in terms of its effect on the state. These effects are expressed by showing the relationship between the state before the operation and the state after the operation has completed. A good high level specification does not need to say how this transformation occurs, only what the end result will be. How precisely we convert the before state to the after state is an implementation issue and there may be many different ways of effecting this transformation. It is considered bad practice to enforce one particular implementation approach.

We now show how the specification of Sugarscape proceeded before discussing how effective this process was. The complete specification is not shown here due to its length but it is available online [27].

Types and Constants. Constants are simply defined by naming the constant and defining its type. Then we state what its specific value is and any invariant properties that it must satisfy. These invariants may relate its value to some other known constants. In some cases we may not wish to state what its value is but only state that it is a constant. For example, the size of the lattice in Sugarscape is a constant size throughout any given simulation run but different values may be used for any one particular run. The simulation size may be chosen based on the amount of available processing power we have available. In this case we state that it is a constant and leave its actual value unstated in the specification. Anyone using the specification must then decide for themselves what size grid they are using and state its value. In this case the grid size is passed in as a parameter by the simulation implementer. These constants act as placeholders that must be given values before the simulation can proceed. By identifying these constants that have not been assigned specific values we have identified (possibly deliberate) ambiguities in the definition of Sugarscape.

$$CULTURECOUNT : \mathbb{N}_1 \qquad\qquad (1a)$$
$$MINMETABOLISM, MAXMETABOLISM : \mathbb{N} \quad (2a)$$
$$M : \mathbb{N}_1 \qquad\qquad (3)$$

$$CULTURECOUNT \bmod 2 = 1 \qquad\qquad (1b)$$
$$MINMETABOLISM < MAXMETABOLISM \qquad (2b)$$

1. $CULTURECOUNT$ (1a) defines the size of the culture string. Although we do not have a specific size for $CULTURECOUNT$ we do know that it must be an odd number (1b) as the culture string is defined to contain an odd number of bits;
2. Similarly although we know that $MINMETABOLISM$ and $MAXMETABOLISM$ (2a) values are not explicitly stated we are told that $MINMETABOLISM$ must be less than $MAXMETABOLISM$ (2b);

3. M is the dimension of the grid. It is up to the modeller to instantiate this to some specific value.

When the simulation is run specific values *must* be assigned to these constants that satisfy the invariants we have given them. We leave these specific values to the implementer to assign but we have flagged what the constants that define any particular instance of Sugarscape are and forced the implementer to give them values within the given constraints.

We often need to define new types in a specification. These new types are generally used to make the specification easier to read and understand as the examples below clearly demonstrate.

$[AGENT]$ (1)
$POSITION == 0 .. M - 1 \times 0 .. M - 1$ (2)
$SEX ::= male \mid female$ (3)
$BIT ::= 0 \mid 1$ (4)
$affiliation ::= red \mid blue$ (5)

1. $AGENT$ is used as a unique identifier for agents. We could just assign each agent a unique natural number but this approach makes our intentions easier to understand and the specification easier to read;
2. $POSITION$ is also used to make specifying the 2D indices within the grid easier to read and more compact;
3. All agents have a sex attribute that can only take one out of two values;
4. BITs are used to encode both culture preferences and diseases of agents;
5. Every agent has a cultural affiliation defined as either belonging to the blue tribe or red tribe.

State. In Z modularisation is achieved by dividing the specification into schemas. In this case we divided the state into two main separate parts or schemas. The first schema defined the information held by the lattice component of the simulation and the second schema defined the information held by the agents in the simulation.

Although Lattice locations can be viewed as a type of agent this division makes the state easier to comprehend and serves a useful purpose as some operations (known as *rules* in Sugarscape terminology) act only on one of these schemas (for example, the *Growback* rule/operation only affects the lattice and not agents).

The Lattice is an $M \times M$ grid or matrix of locations where each location contains amounts of sugar[5] and pollution. Each location can hold up to a maximum amount of sugar where this maximum amount can vary from location to location.

---

[5] We ignore spice here for simplicity. The complete specification includes spice.

Lattice
$$sugar : POSITION \rightarrow \mathbb{N} \tag{1}$$
$$maxSugar : POSITION \rightarrow \mathbb{N} \tag{2}$$
$$pollution : POSITION \rightarrow \mathbb{N} \tag{3}$$

$$\forall x : POSITION \bullet sugar(x) \leq maxSugar(x) \leq MAXSUGAR \tag{4}$$

Taking each part of the schema in turn:

1. _sugar_ is a mapping that stores the amount of sugar stored at each position in the lattice;
2. _maxSugar_ is a mapping that records the maximum amount of sugar that can be stored in (carried by) each position;
3. _pollution_ records the amount of pollution at each location;
4. Every position's sugar level is less than or equal to the maximum allowed amount for that position which is in turn less than or equal to the _MAXSUGAR_ constant;

Each function in the _Lattice_ schema is a total[6] function which means that every position has a sugar level, a maximum level and a pollution amount.

Every agent is situated on a location within the grid and each location is capable of containing only one agent at a time (putting an upper limit on the number of possible agents). Agents are mobile, that is they can move to a new location if a suitable unoccupied location is available. Movement is both discrete and instantaneous, it is possible for an agent to move to a new location instantly while skipping over all intermediate locations. The attributes that every agent has are:

Vision. How far in the four cardinal directions that an agent can see;

Age. Number of turns of the simulation that an agent has been alive;

Maximum Age. Age at which an agent dies;

Sex. Agents are either male or female;

Sugar Level. The amount of sugar that an agent currently holds. There is no limit to how much sugar an agent can hold;

Initial Sugar. The amount of sugar the agent was initialised with on creation;

Metabolism. The amount of energy, defined by sugar (or resource) consumption, used during every turn of the simulation;

Culture Tags. A sequence of bits that represents the culture of an agent;

Children. For each agent we track its children (if any). To apply the Inheritance rule the full list of an agents children is required.

---

[6] Different types of function such as Total, Partial, Injective, etc. are defined within Z and each has its own symbol.

Loans. Under the credit rule agents are allowed lend and/or borrow sugar for set durations and interest rates so we need to track these loans. For each loan we need to know the lender, the borrower, the loan principal and the due date (represented as the step number);

Diseases. Diseases are sequences of bits that can be passed between agents. An agent may carry more than one disease;

Immunity. Each agent has an associated bit sequence that confers immunity against certain diseases. If the bit sequence representing a disease is a subsequence of an agents immunity bit sequence then that agent is considered immune to that disease.

Agents _____

$population : \mathbb{P}\, AGENT$

$position : AGENT \rightarrowtail POSITION$

$sex : AGENT \nrightarrow SEX$

$vision : AGENT \nrightarrow \mathbb{N}_1$

$age : AGENT \nrightarrow \mathbb{N}$

$maxAge : AGENT \nrightarrow \mathbb{N}_1$

$metabolism : AGENT \nrightarrow \mathbb{N}$

$agentSugar : AGENT \nrightarrow \mathbb{N}$

$initialSugar : AGENT \nrightarrow \mathbb{N}$

$agentCulture : AGENT \nrightarrow \text{seq}\, BIT$

$children : AGENT \nrightarrow \mathbb{P}\, AGENT$

$loanBook : AGENT \leftrightarrow (AGENT \times (\mathbb{N}, \mathbb{N}))$

$agentImmunity : AGENT \nrightarrow \text{seq}\, BIT$

$diseases : AGENT \nrightarrow \mathbb{P}\,\text{seq}\, BIT$

_____

$population =$
$\quad \text{dom}\, position = \text{dom}\, sex = \text{dom}\, vision$
$\quad = \text{dom}\, maxAge = \text{dom}\, agentSugar = \text{dom}\, children$
$\quad = \text{dom}\, agentCulture = \text{dom}\, metabolism = \text{dom}\, age$
$\quad = \text{dom}\, agentImmunity = \text{dom}\, diseases$ $\hspace{4em}(1)$

$\text{dom}\, loanBook \subseteq population$ $\hspace{6em}(2)$
$\text{dom}(\text{ran}\, loanBook) \subseteq population$ $\hspace{5em}(3)$
$\forall x, y : AGENT;\ d : \text{seq}\, BIT \bullet$
$x, y \in population \wedge x \neq y \Rightarrow$ $\hspace{6em}(4)$
$\quad ((age(x) \leq maxAge(x) \wedge MINAGE \leq maxAge(x) \leq MAXAGE$
$\quad \wedge\, \# agentCulture(x) = CULTURECOUNT$
$\quad \wedge\, \# agentImmunity(x) = IMMUNITYLENGTH$
$\quad \wedge\, vision(x) \leq MAXVISION$
$\quad \wedge\, MINMETABOLISM \leq metabolism(x) \leq MAXMETABOLISM$
$\quad \wedge\, position(x) = position(y) \Leftrightarrow x = y)$
$d \in \text{ran}\, diseases(x) \Rightarrow \# d < IMUNITYLENGTH$

1. Every existing agent has an associated age, sex, vision, etc. Note that the population holds only the currently existing agent IDs;
2. Only current members of the population can be lenders;
3. Only current members of the population can be borrowers;
4. Every agent in the population is guaranteed to have a current age less than the maximum allowed age for that agent, a maximum age less than or equal to the global $MAXAGE$, a metabolism between the allowed limits and vision less than or equal to the maximum vision. The sequence of bits representing its culture tags is $CULTURECOUNT$ in size while those representing immunity is $IMMUNITYLENGTH$ in size. All diseases are represented by sequences of bits that are shorter than the immunity sequence.

We need to track the number of turns that have occurred in the simulation. Each turn consists of the application of all rules that form part of the simulation. This is specified in the simple *Step* schema below:

$$
\begin{array}{|l}
\underline{\quad Step \quad\quad\quad\quad\quad\quad\quad\quad\quad\quad\quad\quad\quad\quad\quad} \\
\quad step : \mathbb{N} \\
\\
\hline
\end{array}
$$

The entire simulation consists of locations, agents and a counter holding the tick count. We combine them all in the schema *SugarScape*.

$$
\begin{array}{|l}
\underline{\quad SugarScape \quad\quad\quad\quad\quad\quad\quad\quad\quad\quad\quad\quad\quad\quad} \\
\quad Agents \\
\quad Lattice \\
\quad Step \\
\\
\hline
\end{array}
$$

The initial state of the schema when the simulation begins must also be defined.

$$
\begin{array}{|l}
\underline{\quad InitialSugarScape \quad\quad\quad\quad\quad\quad\quad\quad\quad\quad\quad\quad\quad} \\
\quad Sugarscape' \\
\hline
\quad step' = 0 \qquad\qquad\qquad\qquad\qquad\qquad\qquad\qquad\qquad\qquad (1) \\
\quad \#population' = INITIALPOPULATIONSIZE \qquad\qquad\quad (2) \\
\quad loanBook' = \varnothing \qquad\qquad\qquad\qquad\qquad\qquad\qquad\qquad\quad (3) \\
\quad \forall a : AGENT \bullet \qquad\qquad\qquad\qquad\qquad\qquad\qquad\qquad (4) \\
\quad a \in population' \Rightarrow \\
\qquad (age(a) = 0 \wedge diseases'(a) = \varnothing \wedge children'(a) = \varnothing \\
\qquad \wedge INITIALSUGARMIN \leq agentSugar'(a) \leq INITIALSUGARMAX) \\
\qquad \wedge initialSugar'(a) = agentSugar'(a) \\
\\
\hline
\end{array}
$$

1. *step* is set to zero;
2. The population is set to some initial size;
3. There are no loans as yet;
4. Every agent in the starting population has an age of zero, no diseases or children and some initial sugar level within the agreed limits. The other attributes have random values restricted only by the invariants;

It is important to note the use of *primed* variables. If X is a variable then, in any specification defining an operation, X refers to the value of the variable before the operation begins and X' refers to the value of the variable after the operation finishes. Hence in the initial state definition there are only primed variables present as before initialisation begins the variables have no value (i.e. they are uninitialised).

Operations. Each rule in Sugarscape is defined as a separate operation in Z. To show how this proceeds we will show the specification for the *Growback* rule as it is one of the simpler rules. First we show the original rule definition as stated in [12].

Sugarscape Growback$_\alpha$. At each Lattice position, sugar grows back at a rate of α units per time interval up to the capacity at that position.

Growback determines the rate at which location resources are replenished. The integer constant α indicates the amount by which resources grow during a single step or time interval. If $\alpha = \infty$ then each resource returns to its maximum value during each turn, i.e. it is instantly fully replenished after each step. The rule only refers to a single resource, *sugar*, but the book explicitly defines one other resource *spice* and it is clear that generalisations allowing an arbitrary number of resource types to be held at each Lattice position are acceptable.

Since we are dealing only with one resource we only need to define α for this resource. The constant $SUGARGROWTH$ represents α in this rule and we use this to update the sugar level of each position.

Since the maximum carrying level of each resource cannot be exceeded we will set the resource levels to its maximum value if application of the replenishment rate would result in a value greater than this maximum. With these definitions we can express the *Growback* rule in a simple manner. The last line in the schema (see below) does the work of updating the resource levels of every location.

Growback _____
$\Delta Lattice$

_____

$$pollution' = pollution \tag{1}$$
$$maxSugar' = maxSugar \tag{2}$$
$$sugar' = \{x : POSITION \bullet$$
$$x \mapsto min(\{sugar(x) + SUGARGROWTH, maxSugar(x)\})\} \tag{3}$$

---

1. The value of *pollution* after *Growback* finishes is equal to its value before the operation begins (in other words it is unchanged by the operation);
2. Similarly the value of *maxSugar* after *Growback* finishes is equal to its value before the operation begins;
3. The new sugar levels are calculated using a simple formula to become either, (i) the maximum possible level for that location or (ii) the old level plus the *SUGARGROWTH* whichever is the smaller.

The *Movement* rule in Sugarscape is the best known rule as a similar rule is defined in almost all other ABMs.

Movement - M

– Look out as far as vision permits in each of the four lattice directions, north, south, east and west;
– Considering only unoccupied lattice positions, find the nearest position producing maximum welfare;
– Move to the new position
– Collect all resources at that location

The previous rule affected only the locations but most of the remaining rules affect agents as well as locations. The Movement rule determines how agents select their next location. There are a number of different versions of this rule. We will specify the simplest rule here as it is the only movement rule explicitly defined in the appendix of the Sugarscape book. We add a subscript to the rule title (M_{basic}) to distinguish between the different movement rule specifications.

Not explicitly stated within the rule but stated as a footnote to the rule is the restriction that the order in which the lattice directions are searched should be random. This comes into play when two or more available sites exist with the same welfare score.

This rule does not guarantee that an agent will move to the best location. To see why this is the case consider what happens if two agents both try to move to the same location. Only one can succeed and the other will have to move to a less advantageous location. How we decide which agent succeeds is not defined. We assume that either a conflict resolution or conflict avoidance rule is available to make this decision but it is not stated what this rule should be. The original implementation is sequential with agents assumed to be moving in a random order thus enforcing collision avoidance. No guidance is provided for concurrent implementations.

To help make the specification clear we define some simple helper functions. The distance between two positions is only defined for positions that are directly horizontal or vertical to each other. This function must take into account the torus-like (wrap around) structure of the simulation.

$distance : POSITION \times POSITION$
$\rightarrow \mathbb{N}$

$\forall\, x1, x2, y1, y2 : \mathbb{N} \bullet$
$distance((x1, y1), (x1, y2)) = \qquad (1)$
$\quad min(\{|\, y2 - y1\,|, M-\,|\, y2 - y1\,|\})$
$distance((x1, y1), (x2, y2)) = \qquad (2)$
$\quad min(\{|\, x1 - x2\,|, M-\,|\, x1 - x2\,|\})$
$distance((x1, y1), (x2, y2)) = \infty \Leftrightarrow$
$\quad x1 \neq x2 \wedge y1 \neq y2 \qquad (3)$

1. If two agents are vertically aligned we calculate distance based on the horizontal distance;
2. If two agents are horizontally aligned we calculate distance based on the vertical distance;
3. Otherwise the distance is defined as ∞.

We use this to define the *adjacent* function that lets us know if two agents are directly beside each other.

$adjacent : POSITION \times POSITION$
$\rightarrow boolean$

$\forall\, a, b : POSITION \bullet$
$adjacent(a, b) \Leftrightarrow distance(a, b) = 1$

visibleAgents takes an agent, a function mapping agents to positions and the vision range of the agent and returns the set of agents that are within that agent's neighbourhood.

$visibleAgents : AGENT$
$\quad \times (AGENT \nrightarrow POSITION)$
$\quad \times \mathbb{N}$
$\nrightarrow \mathbb{F}\, AGENT$

$\forall\, agent : AGENT;\ pos : AGENT \nrightarrow POSITION;\ range : \mathbb{N} \bullet$
$visibleAgents(agent, pos, range) =$
$\quad \{ag : AGENT \mid ag \in \mathrm{dom}\, pos \wedge 1 \leq distance(pos(ag), pos(agent)) \leq range\}$

$Movement_{basic}$ ─────────────────────────
$\Delta SugarScape$

$step' = step$
$population' = population$
$maxSugar' = maxSugar$
$pollution' = pollution$
$sex' = sex$
$vision' = vision$
$age' = age$
$maxAge' = maxAge$
$agentCulture' = agentCulture$
$loanBook' = loanBook$
$diseases' = diseases$
$agentImmunity' = agentImmunity$
$children' = children$
$metabolism' = metabolism$
$initialSugar' = initialSugar$
$\forall a : AGENT; l : POSITION \bullet$
$a \in population' \Rightarrow$ $\hspace{5cm}$ (1)
$\quad distance(position'(a), position(a)) \leq vision(a)$

$(distance(position(a), l) \leq vision(a) \wedge (l \notin \text{ran } position')) \Rightarrow$ $\hspace{1cm}$ (2)
$\quad sugar(l) \leq sugar(position'(a))$ $\hspace{4.5cm}$ (2a)
$\quad \wedge \ (distance(l, position(a)) < distance(position'(a), position(a)))$ (2b)
$\quad\quad \Rightarrow sugar(l) < sugar(position'(a))$

$agentSugar' = \{\forall a : AGENT \mid a \in population' \bullet$
$\quad a \mapsto agentSugar(a) + sugar(position'(a))\}$ $\hspace{3cm}$ (3)
$sugar' = sugar \oplus \{\forall l : POSITION \mid l \in \text{ran } position' \bullet l \mapsto 0\}$ $\hspace{0.5cm}$ (4)

After the rule is applied the following will be the case for every agent:

1. Each agent will be located within one of the locations in their original neighbourhood (possibly the same position as before);
2. After every agent has moved:
   (a) There will exist no remaining available locations from the original neighbourhood of an agent that would have given a better welfare score than the location that agent now inhabits (we picked the maximum reward);
   (b) If there was more than one location with maximum reward then the agent moved to the closest location.
3. Agent sugar levels increase because they consume all the sugar at their new location (even if the new location is the same as their old location);
4. Location sugar levels are set to zero everywhere there is an agent present.

The specification states what is true after the application of the rule but not how we achieve that state. In any implementation some conflict resolution strategy will be needed but in this specification we remain agnostic as to what it should be.

The rule is well stated but requires that we precisely define *welfare*. For a single resource simulation welfare is precisely equal to the amount of sugar available at a location.

The remaining rules are specified in a similar manner. The complete specification contains rule variants where a rule has more than one definition (as is the case with *Movement*). In line with the original simulation definition each rule is also defined under an asynchronous updating strategy for the sake of completeness.

6.2   Results of the Specification

Formally specifying Sugarscape allowed us to identify a number of issues with its definition. We have grouped these issues into three main categories: *Lack of Clarity*, *Missing Information* and *Sequential biases.*

Lack of Clarity. The rules, although simply stated, lack clarity in their definition. Only one version of each rule is presented even when many variations are referred to in the text. The variations presented cannot always be used together, for example the *Movement* rule defined in the appendix is not the variant required if the pollution rule is also used. Our specification brings all the variants together in one place for ease of reference. We also identified the combinations of rules that are allowable within any particular simulation setup.

Missing Information. Missing or incomplete information is the biggest cause for concern. In many cases we can work out the most likely answer based on context but in some cases there is not one definitive correct answer. If there was more than one arguably correct solution we choose the simplest. How we fill in these blanks can have a big effect on how the simulation proceeds. These effects may be important if we are trying to compare different implementations of Sugarscape. For example, there is no mention of any minimum amount required by agents to have children in the *Mating* rule but such an amount is referenced in the *Credit* rule.

By replacing each ambiguous interpretation with one simple and precise interpretation we allow different developers to replicate and benchmark their results against each other. All hidden assumptions that could serve to advantage one implementation over another or lead to different simulation outcomes are excised.

Sequential Biases. Sugarscape is based on the assumption that it will be implemented sequentially. While this was a good assumption at the time it was written it is not now necessarily the case. Improvements in processing speed have recently been attained mainly through the introduction of concurrency. Simulations are now almost always run on multicore or even multiprocessor machines.

Building assumptions about the processor architecture into the simulation definition is not good practice. A properly defined simulation should be independent of such implementation concerns.

The Z specification is free from all sequential assumptions. It achieves this without having to specify or constrain in any way what conflict resolution or avoidance strategies are employed. This leaves developers the freedom to try out different approaches as suits their implementation platform. However modellers still need to explicitly and clearly state what particular resolution strategies they are employing as these can alter the simulation outcomes.

Although the original Sugarscape definition explicitly assumes that the implementation will be a sequential one we have chosen not to make this assumption in our specification.

To be sure this assumption can be included in the specification and we have produced an alternative explicitly sequential specification of *Combat* for comparison. To allow comparisons to be made between the synchronous and asynchronous versions of Sugarscape we have produced an alternative asynchronous updating specification of each rule of Sugarscape[7]. We note that explicitly demanding asynchronous updating be used does have a large affect on the structure of the specification. While this is not unexpected as it is well known that asynchronous and synchronous updating give different outcomes in simulations [6,7,23,37] it is worth noting that two separate formal specifications are required to distinguish between asynchronous and synchronous updating.

6.3   Conclusions

Of the thirteen rules of Sugarscape our specification process found issues in all but four of the rules (Growback, Pollution Formation, Culture and Trade). It is interesting to note that although *Trade* is probably the most complex rule there were no issues with its definition. This may be because it is a self-contained rule unaffected by the other rules. The more interesting issues were due to the unforeseen interactions that can occur between rules. For example, when *Credit* and *Inheritance* are used together in a simulation it is unclear how we deal with loans of dead agents. Are they inherited by the children or discarded? Similarly *Credit* mentions using the minimum amount required by agents to have children to help calculate loan amounts but this minimum amount is not mentioned in the *Mating* rule. The ambiguities and missing information within the other nine rules have a significant effect on the outcome of a simulation run. This helps to explain why Sugarscape has proven so difficult to replicate.

Further work remains to be done in getting agreement from the ABM community on the decisions made in producing this interpretation of Sugarscape. Any incorrect assumptions made in the course of producing this specification need to be identified, agreed upon and corrected. A more complete list of the issues identified during the specification process can be found in [27].

---

[7] Apart from Pollution Diffusion which is explicitly defined synchronously.

Sugarscape can now be used as a benchmark (or rather set of benchmarks) for modellers. This is particularly useful for those proposing alternative approaches to simulation such as synchronous updating or comparing the performance gains under different processor architectures, for example, Multicore versus Graphics Processor Units (GPU).

7   Issues with Formal Specification

We have demonstrated that formal methods can be used to specify even a complex ABM such as Sugarscape. The fact that it identified many ambiguities shows that it fulfils its purpose. Formal methods have many years of solid research and a strong theoretical grounding behind them. They are designed to make specification of large and complex systems as easy as possible by building in modularity.

Our Sugarscape specification shows that we can model an ABM at a very high level while still remaining very precise. This is a key issue as we need a way of specifying our simulations that allows not just replicability but more importantly reproducibility. The benefit is that the specification does not force us to adopt one particular set of parameters but it does force us to state precisely what values we have attached to those parameters.

There are, of course, downsides to the use of formal specification. The price we pay for their precision is a requirement for mathematical formalisms that some modellers may find too difficult or time consuming. To quote a well known paper in computer science "there is no silver bullet" [5]. The quest for a simple and intuitive natural language-based specification technique has proven futile in computer science and will similarly prove futile here. If we want reproducibility then we need the rigour of mathematics. The size of the formal specification produced for Sugarscape may seem large but we must remember that:

- it is an entire family of simulations with very complex interactions;
- we have specified it twice, once with a single resource (Sugar) and once with two resources (Sugar and Spice). Most other ABSS are smaller and simpler in scope and would require less work;
- we have specified Asynchronous and Synchronous versions of each rule.

While the Z notation allowed us to produce an acceptable specification of Sugarscape there are other more recently developed specification languages such as Alloy [25] or Object-Z [38] that may prove even more effective and produce simpler specifications. Translating from Z to these other notations would allow for a fair comparison to be made between the different specification techniques. Formal specification deserves serious consideration as an approach to solving the replicability issue in ABM. While some may feel it is "overkill" for normal specification there is a stronger case for its use in specifications used as benchmarks, comparisons of updating techniques (synchronous vs asynchronous) or implementation techniques on GPU/multicore architectures.

Formal methods are difficult and time consuming to read and/or write. Both tasks require a familiarity of the underlying mathematics and the available tools.

While reading and understanding an existing specification is not as onerous as writing one some mathematical sophistication is still required. It may be the case that computer scientists will be needed to produce these specifications for modellers and also to aid in implementing them until modellers become more familiar with the mathematics underlying formal specification techniques. This should come as no surprise: software development is a highly skilled task. Formal methods are not an easy solution to the problem but then decades of research in computer science indicate that there is no easy solution (no "silver bullet") to this problem. Formal methods do not guarantee correctness but they do reduce the ambiguity of the ABM description, make errors easier to spot and models verifiable. Any attempted solution to this problem will require hard work and a firm mathematical foundation.

8   Implementing Sugarscape

8.1   Framework Details

The framework is a proof of concept implementation of Synchronous Updating algorithms for ABM that also implements Asynchronous updating. This framework is designed in a manner that allows different strategies to be attached to a single implementation of any rule thereby guaranteeing that the only difference between the implementations is the updating strategy employed. It was developed in C++11 on OS X and Linux. As the framework primarily serves as a reference implementation the code has been kept as simple as possible. Whenever a choice existed between efficiency and clarity, clarity was chosen. The framework is documented using the *DOxygen* documentation tool [40]. Full source code and documentation is licensed under the GPLv3 and is available online [28].

The framework implements a number of different existing Asynchronous Updating strategies alongside a new Synchronous algorithm. Specifically three different Asynchronous Updating strategies are implemented:

Fixed Direction Line-By-Line. The locations in the lattice representing the simulation space are updated in the order they appear in the lattice (left to right, top-down);

Fixed Random Sweep. The order that is used is determined randomly at the start of the simulation and this order is used for every step in the simulation;

Random New Sweep. The order that the agents are updated is determined randomly at the start of each step (each step uses a different random order).

Where a rule contains some random element (such as randomly choosing between different locations when deciding where to move to) the *Mersenne Twister* [32] Pseudo Random Number Generator is employed. All other issues, such as contention or concurrency, are handled transparently by the framework. This allows the framework to be used to produce side by side comparisons between the contrasting synchronous and asynchronous updating strategies. Something that is not generally undertaken within ABSS.

At present we have developed the single resource version of the Sugarscape simulation. The single resource version employs 12 of the 13 rules. The final rule *Trade* requires a second resource type, known as *Spice*, so that *Sugar* can be traded against *Spice*. Although this means that the *Trade* rule is not implemented, the 12 implemented rules cover the full range of interaction types including 8 rules with a complexity equivalent to *Trade* (e.g. *Combat* and *Culture*).

The framework consists of two applications. The first contains a simple Viewport GUI developed with the freely available and open source SFML (*Simple and Fast Multimedia Library*) [16]. The viewport GUI is used for viewing agent behaviour in real time on the screen. The *viewport* provided is very simple and was used when implementing the framework to ensure that the various Sugarscape behaviours made sense, that is, to help judge their correctness. One example of its use would be to look for characteristic waves of agent migration between sugar peaks on the lattice as described in *Growing Artificial Societies* [12]. The second application contains no GUI. This was used when we required data logging of specific simulation attributes over time as in, for example, measuring the population count of the simulation over time.

8.2 Results Obtained

There is no general agreement on what the original parameters of Sugarscape were and, as we have shown with our formal specification of Sugarscape, there are many ambiguities. This makes it impossible to show that any particular interpretation of the specification completely matches the original and thus makes comparisons between different implementations difficult. That being said, now that we have a formal specification of Sugarscape, this can be used as a reference for checking the effects of different updating strategies on the simulation outcomes. Where any particular result is not reproducible it is possible, based on the formal specification, to pinpoint the ambiguities that make reproduction of this result impossible.

We have made our definitions match the originals as closely as possible. Where the detail is precise it is replicated precisely and where there is ambiguity a best guess was made and documented of the original authors intentions. However, even given these ambiguities we can still see if we can replicate the general emergent properties and trends in the simulation[8].

Given the previous work on the differences between updating strategies in Cellular Automata some differences in the simulation outcomes were expected. What was not known was how big or important these differences will be. The comparisons shown here provide new insights into this.

In general terms we found that:

1. In most cases, where sufficient information is available in the original simulation definition, it is possible to reproduce previous results;

---

[8] That is, trends in population growth, spread of culture over time, etc.

2. When results are not reproducible the formal specification precisely identifies the parameters used and the ambiguities or missing information from the original simulation definition;
3. The use of different updating strategies adds confidence to any results obtained by ensuring results are not due to "artefacts" in the updating process. It also gives confidence in any results obtained even when those results do not agree with the original results that are being replicated. This extra assurance is invaluable.

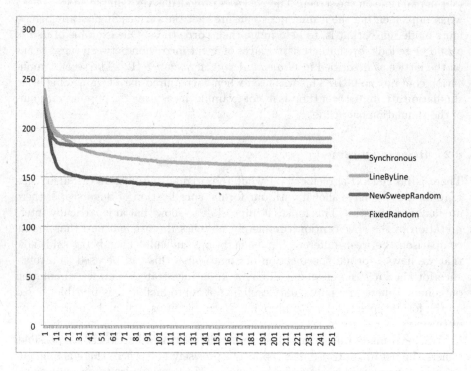

Fig. 1. Lattice carrying capacity: Updating strategies compared

Although there were some slight differences in the simulation outcomes when comparing synchronous with asynchronous updating the emergent properties remained consistent. One such example is the difference in carrying capacity of the lattice when synchronous updating is employed (see Fig. 1). When we compare the carrying capacity of the simulation under the different updating strategies we can see that although they all have the same distinctive shape there are some differences between them. The original sugarscape updating strategy was *Random New Sweep*, the most commonly employed updating strategy in ABM and ABSS. This shows that the properties of Sugarscape appear to be independent of updating strategy, strengthening the original findings from Sugarscape.

The one notable case where we could not replicate the original results was population stability with sexual reproduction. It was originally shown that the population is stable under sexual reproduction with only small periodic oscillations in population size. Despite replicating the original setup as closely as possible we were unable to repeat this result. In all cases the population (under all updating strategies) collapsed before 2,500 steps had passed (see Fig. 2).

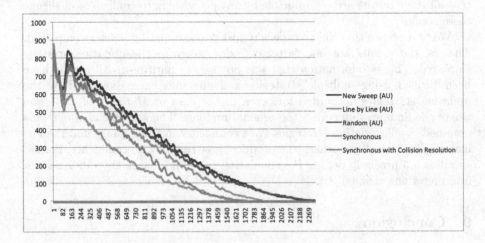

Fig. 2. Population collapse with G_1, M, and S

The only unknown in the simulation setup is the initial lattice setup. Although we have replicated this as closely as possible, given the information available, without the original details we cannot know how close we are to the original (or not). This missing information was enough to derail our replication of the original result.

A closer examination of the simulation parameters shows why it is difficult to get a stable population. Female agents are fertile for at most 35 time steps. A stable population requires females to have an average of just over two offspring in their lifetime. Since having a child halves an agents resources the agent must then regain these resources at a rate that allows them a chance of having one or possibly two more children within those 35 steps. If the balance among the simulation parameters is wrong and agents are unable to have two children or more children within their timespan then the population will collapse. Similarly if they have too many children then the population explosion will deplete the lattice of sugar and result in a population collapse. The operational parameters we gleaned from our reading of Sugarscape does not appear to have the required balance. This part of the simulation needs to be revisited and clarified before reproduction of the original results is possible. Even here where we could not attain the desired results the precise specification should enable others to pinpoint any errors we made with greater ease.

Based on our formal specification we have successfully reproduced many of the results originally shown in [12]. Where reproduction was not possible the use of different updating strategies gave us confidence in our findings. Our formal specification allowed us to identify the weaknesses in the original simulation specification that makes those results difficult to reproduce. This shows the efficacy of using formal methods in ABM and ABSS. The production of a formal specification of the simulation [27] alongside the freely available code [28] means that all these results are reproducible by anyone wishing to confirm or challenge these results.

We have shown that Sugarscape is robust to the updating strategy employed. That is, the results are not "artefacts" due solely to the updating strategy employed. This is information that was not known until now. All results have been verified using multiple strategies and any differences produced by the updating strategies accounted for, even in the case of *Mating and Evolution* where the findings differ from the original findings. The agreement in outcome obtained by all updating strategies gives confidence in the findings and the formal specification allows others to reproduce these results with confidence. Formal specification precisely defines the simulation rules and makes any differences in interpretations visible.

9   Conclusion

It is recognised that there is an issue with replication in ABM and as has been pointed out [9,33] replication is not the same as reproduction. Simply forcing authors to publish their model's implementation will not give us reproducibility. If their models are incorrect then just replicating them will just replicate their errors. What is required is more along the lines of the model-driven approach [11] where a conceptually high level model independent of implementation details is provided. The inclusion of extra data alongside the published results [22] will obviously help but it is not enough. We should be able to reproduce their results, based on their model, using our own implementations.

What is missing is the ability to specify the model in a clear and precise manner such that independent replication of an implementation becomes possible and ambiguities and errors in the model can be revealed. One approach in computer science that fits this criteria is formal methods where the model is specified with mathematical rigour and can, if necessary, be formally verified.

Although [11] states that experimentation is the only way to verify a model this does not preclude but rather requires some precise specification of the model so we can prove that an implementation of the model is a correct interpretation of this model.

We have produced a formal specification of the Sugarscape family of simulations [27]. It is, to the best of our knowledge, the first formal specification of the entire Sugarscape simulation family. The purpose of the specification is to provide a clear, unambiguous and precise definition of Sugarscape and demonstrate the applicability of formal methods to helping solve the replication problem.

The specification has identified many ambiguities and/or missing information in the original rule definitions. Where there was an obvious way of removing these ambiguities we have done so. If there was more than one possible solution we chose the most likely one.

Because our specification is high level and only defines the before and after state of each rule it makes no assumptions as to how any rule will be implemented. All inherent biases towards, for example, a sequential implementation have been rmade completely explicit. Implementers have complete freedom as to what programming model they employ (Object-oriented, imperative, functional, or any concurrent approach). Any simulations that adhere to the specification can be properly compared in terms of performance or patterns of behaviour. This will put on a firmer foundation any claims made by researchers about their implementations.

We used the specification to provide a reference implementation of Sugarscape [28] that employs both synchronous and asynchronous updating. It demonstrates the robustness of Sugarcape to the updating strategy employed. Using this framework and the formal specification we have shown that although different updating strategies affect aspects of the simulation outcomes the overall emergent properties of the simulation appear to be independent of the particular strategy employed [29].

Specifying Sugarscape has made a huge difference to our understanding of the simulation and although it took some time to write we feel that it has, in the end, saved time by identifying issues in advance of implementation and giving the simulation a clarity that enables it to be used by others. While we could have implemented our synchronous Sugarscape framework without first formally specifying it the specification process ensured that we had a fuller understanding of the simulation. Any problems or ambiguities were found and clarified before we started coding thus making the code cleaner and simpler.

Formal Specification produces a high level conceptual model of a system. It is mathematically precise and allows for correctness properties of a system to be proven. This high level approach abstracts away implementation details thus allowing the model to be precise without being over prescriptive. It is precisely these properties that make formal methods suitable for the development of safety critical systems. In our case we specified Sugarscape under many different updating strategies. Formal specification has also been shown to lead to fewer errors in any resulting code.

While model alignment and reimplementation are powerful tools in replication they can only be effective if there is an agreed high level and precise conceptual model to align. Currently formal methods remain the gold standard in computer science for the production of specifications that match these characteristics.

While we believe that the Z notation is not the best formal method to use, it is well known and many newer methods more suited to ABM are based on it [25,38]. Our Z specification can be translated into any one of the newer methods by their advocates without much difficulty.

The specification itself is complex. Specifying the single resource scenario took 46 pages of Z with embedded explanatory text. Researchers not familiar with Z or its underlying mathematics may find it difficult to understand. It is an open question as to whether the benefits of formally specifying an ABM is sufficient to repay the amount of effort required to produce it.

Specifying systems precisely is difficult. Computer science has been engaged in this issue for decades and is still trying to solve the problem. There is no easy solution. In terms of precision, formal specifications are unbeatable as they are embedded in a firm mathematical foundation. Formally specifying an ABM is no small undertaking and requires a familiarity with mathematical topics that some modellers may not presently be familiar with. For some models the use of formal methods may be overkill but in some cases, for example, when a model is used as a benchmark for testing toolkit usability or approaches to employing concurrency within ABM there is a stronger case to be made for their usage.

If modellers want reproducibility then they must treat their ABM specifications as first class citizens and demand the same precision from them as they do from other aspects of their models. We have shown that formal methods, even *formal methods-lite* can be used to uncover problems and help tackle the replication problem within ABM.

9.1   Further Work

This specification has been made available [27] for anyone who wishes to use it and provides a standard reference that researchers can use when producing their own implementation.

It will prove invaluable, for example, to researchers who advocate the use of a GPU [8,31,35], containing hundreds to thousands of individual processors, for improved performance. The more complex rules in Sugarscape (such as Combat, Inheritance and Mating) are not easily parallelized and provide a better test of how well parallelisation algorithms work than other simpler rules. By providing this precise and complete definition of these rules it is now possible for researchers to properly compare how different models cope with the more complex and realistic ABMs.

This implementation is also being used to benchmark the concurrent performance of novel synchronous updating algorithms for ABM on multicore and GPU architectures.

Acknowledgements. The Institute of Technology Carlow provided partial support for this work.

References

1. Abdallah, A.E., Jones, C.B., Sanders, J.W. (eds.): Communicating Sequential Processes. The First 25 Years. LNCS, vol. 3525. Springer, Heidelberg (2005). doi:10.1007/b136154

2. Berryman, M.: Review of software platforms for agent based models. Technical report, DTIC Document (2008)
3. Bigbee, A., Cioffi-Revilla, C., Luke, S.: Replication of Sugarscape Using MASON. Springer, Tokyo (2007). doi:10.1007/978-4-431-71307-4_20
4. Bjørner, D., Havelund, K.: 40 years of formal methods. In: Jones, C., Pihlajasaari, P., Sun, J. (eds.) FM 2014. LNCS, vol. 8442, pp. 42–61. Springer, Cham (2014). doi:10.1007/978-3-319-06410-9_4
5. Brooks, F.P.: No silver bullet essence and accidents of software engineering. Computer **20**(4), 10–19 (1987)
6. Caron-Lormier, G., Humphry, R.W., Bohan, D.A., Hawes, C., Thorbek, P.: Asynchronous and synchronous updating in individual-based models. Ecol. Model. **212**(3–4), 522–527 (2008)
7. Cornforth, D., Green, D.G., Newth, D.: Ordered asynchronous processes in multiagent systems. Phys. D Nonlinear Phenom. **204**(1–2), 70–82 (2005)
8. Deissenberg, C., van der Hoog, S., Dawid, H.: EURACE: a massively parallel agentbased model of the European economy. Appl. Math. Comput. **204**(2), 541–552 (2008). Special Issue on New Approaches in Dynamic Optimization to Assessment of Economic and Environmental Systems
9. Drummond, C.: Replicability is not reproducibility: nor is it good science (2009)
10. D'Souza, R.M., Lysenko, M., Rahmani, K.: SugarScape on steroids: simulating over a million agents at interactive rates. In: Proceedings of Agent 2007 (2007)
11. Edmonds, B., Hales, D.: Replication, replication and replication: some hard lessons from model alignment. J. Artif. Soc. Soc. Simul. **6**(4) (2003)
12. Epstein, J.M., Axtell, R.: Growing Artificial Societies: Social Science from the Bottom Up. The Brookings Institution, Washington, DC (1996)
13. AM, et al.: CZT: Community z toolS. http://czt.sourceforge.net/. Accessed 30 Sept 2015
14. Galan, J.M., Izquierdo, L.R., Izquierdo, S.S., Santos, J.I., Olmo, R.D., Lopez-Paredes, A., Edmonds, B.: Errors and artefacts in agent-based modelling (2009)
15. Gilbert, N.: Private communication, March 2014
16. Gomila, L.: Simple and fast multimedia library (2015)
17. Grimm, V., Berger, U., Bastiansen, F., Eliassen, S., Ginot, V., Giske, J., Goss-Custard, J., Grand, T., Heinz, S.K., Huse, G., Huth, A., Jepsen, J.U., Jørgensen, C., Mooij, W.M., Müller, B., Pe'er, G., Piou, C., Railsback, S.F., Robbins, A.M., Robbins, M.M., Rossmanith, E., Rüger, N., Strand, E., Souissi, S., Stillman, R.A., Vabø, R., Visser, U., DeAngelis, D.L.: A standard protocol for describing individual-based and agent-based models. Ecol. Model. **198**(1–2), 115–126 (2006)
18. Grimm, V., Berger, U., DeAngelis, D.L., Polhill, J.G., Giske, J., Railsback, S.F.: The ODD protocol: a review and first update. Ecol. Model. **221**(23), 2760–2768 (2010)
19. Hinkelmann, F., Murrugarra, D., Jarrah, A., Laubenbacher, R.: A mathematical framework for agent based models of complex biological networks. Bull. Math. Biol. **73**(7), 1583–1602 (2011)
20. Hinsen, K.: A data and code model for reproducible research and executable papers. Procedia Comput. Sci. **4**, 579–588 (2011). Proceedings of the International Conference on Computational Science, ICCS 2011
21. Hinsen, K.: Computational science: shifting the focus from tools to models. F1000Research **3**, 101 (2014)
22. Hinsen, K.: Activepapers: a platform for publishing and archiving computer-aided research. F1000Research **3**, 289 (2015)

23. Huberman, B.A., Glance, N.S.: Evolutionary games and computer simulations. Proc. Natl. Acad. Sci. **90**(16), 7716–7718 (1993)
24. Inchiosa, M.E., Parker, M.T.: Overcoming design and development challenges in agent-based modeling using ascape. Proc. Natl. Acad. Sci. **99**(suppl 3), 7304–7308 (2002)
25. Jackson, D.: Software Abstractions: Logic, Language, and Analysis. The MIT Press, Cambridge (2006)
26. Jones, C.B.: Systematic Software Development Using VDM, 2nd edn. Prentice Hall International, Englewood Cliffs (1990)
27. Kehoe, J.: The specification of sugarscape (2015). http://arxiv.org/abs/1505.06012
28. Kehoe, J.: Synchronous sugarscape: a reference implementation (2015). https://github.com/josephkehoe/Sugarscape. Accessed 30 Dec 2015
29. Kehoe, J.: Robust reproducibility of agent based models. In: The European Simulation and Modelling Conference. Inderscience, October 2016
30. Kitchin, J.R.: Examples of effective data sharing in scientific publishing. ACS Catal. **5**, 3894–3899 (2015)
31. Lysenko, M., D'Souza, R.: A framework for megascale agent based model simulations on graphics processing units. J. Artif. Soc. Soc. Simul. **11**(4) (2008)
32. Matsumoto, M., Nishimura, T.: Mersenne twister: A 623-dimensionally equidistributed uniform pseudo-random number generator. ACM Trans. Model. Comput. Simul. **8**(1), 3–30 (1998)
33. Peng, R.D.: Reproducible research in computational science. Science (New York, NY) **334**(6060), 1226–1227 (2011)
34. Railsback, S.F., Lytinen, S.L., Jackson, S.K.: Agent-based simulation platforms: review and development recommendations. Simulation **82**(9), 609–623 (2006)
35. Richmond, P., Coakley, S., Romano, D.M.: A high performance agent based modelling framework on graphics card hardware with CUDA. In: Proceedings of the 8th International Conference on Autonomous Agents and Multiagent Systems, AAMAS 2009, Richland, SC, vol. 2, pp. 1125–1126. International Foundation for Autonomous Agents and Multiagent Systems (2009)
36. Sansores, C., Pavón, J.: Agent-based simulation replication: a model driven architecture approach. In: Gelbukh, A., Albornoz, Á., Terashima-Marín, H. (eds.) MICAI 2005. LNCS (LNAI), vol. 3789, pp. 244–253. Springer, Heidelberg (2005). doi:10.1007/11579427_25
37. Schönfisch, B., de Roos, A.: Synchronous and asynchronous updating in cellular automata. Biosystems **51**(3), 123–143 (1999)
38. Smith, G.: The Object-Z Specification Language, vol. 1. Springer, New York (2012). doi:10.1007/978-1-4615-5265-9
39. Spivey, J.M.: The Z Notation: A Reference Manual. Prentice-Hall, Inc., Upper Saddle River (1989)
40. van Heesch, D.: Doxygen (2015)
41. Woodcock, J., Larsen, P.G., Bicarregui, J., Fitzgerald, J.: Formal methods: practice and experience. ACM Comput. Surv. **41**(4), 19:1–19:36 (2009)

Summarizing Simulation Results
Using Causally-Relevant States

Nidhi Parikh$^{(\boxtimes)}$, Madhav Marathe, and Samarth Swarup

Network Dynamics and Simulation Science Lab,
Biocomplexity Institute of Virginia Tech, Virginia Tech, Blacksburg, VA, USA
nidhip@lanl.gov, {mmarathe,swarup}@bi.vt.edu

Abstract. As increasingly large-scale multiagent simulations are being
implemented, new methods are becoming necessary to make sense of the
results of these simulations. Even summarizing the results of a given simulation run is a challenge. Here we pose this as the problem of simulation
summarization: how to extract the causally-relevant descriptions of the
trajectories of the agents in the simulation. We present a simple algorithm to compress agent trajectories through state space by identifying
the state transitions which are relevant to determining the distribution
of outcomes at the end of the simulation. We present a couple of toy-
examples to illustrate how the algorithm works, and then we apply it to
a complex simulation of a major disaster in an urban area.

Keywords: Simulation summarization · Causal states

1 Introduction

Large-scale multiagent simulations are becoming increasingly common in many
domains of scientific interest, including epidemiology [9], disaster response [23],
and urban planning [22]. These simulations have complex models of agents, environments, infrastructures, and interactions. Often the goal is to study a hypothetical situation or a counter-factual scenario in a detailed and realistic virtual
setting, with the intention of making policy recommendations.

In practice, this is done through a statistical experimental design, where a
parameter space is explored through multiple simulation runs and the outcomes
are compared for statistically significant differences.

As simulations get larger and more complex, however, we encounter two kinds
of situations where it is difficult to apply this methodology. First, if a simulation
is too computationally intensive to run enough number of times, we don't obtain
the statistical power necessary to find significant differences between the cells
in a statistical experiment design. Second, if the interventions are not actually

---

This paper is being reused and has already appeared in Parikh N., Marathe
M., Swarup S. (2016) Summarizing Simulation Results Using Causally-Relevant
States. In: Osman N., Sierra C. (eds.) Autonomous Agents and Multiagent Systems.
AAMAS 2016. Lecture Notes in Computer Science, vol 10003. Springer, Cham.

L.G. Nardin and L. Antunes (Eds.): MABS 2016, LNAI 10399, pp. 71–91, 2017.
DOI: 10.1007/978-3-319-67477-3_4

known ahead of time, we don't even know how to create a statistical experiment. In this situation, the goal of the simulation is to get some insights about effects of various behaviors in different contexts. This can potentially help design a policy which can then be evaluated using the same model.

New methodologies and new techniques are needed for the analysis of such complex simulations. Part of the problem is that large-scale multiagent simulations can generate much more data in each simulation run than goes into the simulation, i.e., we end up with more data than we started with. In addition, the data may be highly correlated. Sense-making in this regime is a challenge.

As a first step towards addressing these kinds of problems, we introduce the problem of simulation summarization. The goal of this problem is to come up with a summary description of a single large multiagent simulation run. The method we introduce is based on a theory of causal states in stochastic processes (see Sect. 3). It is simple to implement, which is essential when applying to very large simulations, and is actually more meaningful the larger the simulation, since larger numbers of agents give more statistical power.

The rest of this paper is organized as follows. First we describe the simulation summarization problem and discuss some related work. Then we review the idea of causal states for extracting patterns from time series data. After that we describe how we adapt this idea to the analysis of the results of large-scale simulations. Then we present a couple of toy examples to illustrate the effectiveness of our method, before applying it to a large and complex simulation of an improvised nuclear detonation in an urban area. We show how our method identifies a number of meaningful causal patterns in the simulation results, while also greatly compressing the results. We end with a discussion of applications and extensions of our method.

2   Problem Description

What constitutes a good summary? This is a question that has been studied in domains such as natural language processing where the goal is to summarize a document or a corpus [16,17], but, as far as we know, is entirely novel for multiagent simulations.

Our perspective on summarizing a multiagent simulation outputs is that the summary representation should capture the causally-relevant states of the simulation. We use the phrase "causally-relevant" instead of causal to side-step the well-known problems with finding causality. There are many efforts aimed at establishing (various forms of) causality in data [11–13,21]. Our goal here is not to establish causality, but to compress the simulation results while retaining meaningful states. The intuition is that finding causally-relevant states of the simulation is the most meaningful way to compress it.

In line with this intuition, we adapt the approach of "causal states" that has been developed over the last several years, as reviewed in the next section. By "causally-relevant", in this context, we mean agent states that are maximally informative about outcomes of interest.

Even in simulation scenarios where the set of interventions or cases to study is not known *a priori*, i.e., simulations which are intended to be exploratory in nature, there is a set of outcomes we care about. For instance, in a disaster simulation we explore in Sect. 6, the outcome of interest is the health of the agents. Causally-relevant states in this simulation are all the states which have a measurable impact on agent health, even if the impact is delayed. For example in this simulation, being exposed to radiation has an impact on health state only after several hours have passed. The summary should be able to reveal that it is the exposure to radiation that is the causally-relevant state, not the actual change in the agent's health state (since that follows deterministically once exposure has happened).

Next we describe the formalism of causal states which is more broadly applicable to stochastic processes before turning to our approach for simulation summarization.

3   Causal States

Crutchfield and others have developed the theory of minimal causal representations of stochastic processes, termed computational mechanics [7,18]. We briefly review the concepts here before describing how we have adapted them for the summarization problem.

Consider a stochastic process as a sequence of random variables X_t, drawn from a discrete alphabet, $\mathcal{A}$. We will write $\overleftarrow{X}$ to denote the *past* of the sequence, i.e., the sequence $X_{-\infty} \ldots X_{t-2} X_{t-1} X_t$, and $\overrightarrow{X}$ to denote the *future* of the sequence, i.e., the sequence $X_{t+1} X_{t+2} \ldots X_\infty$, following [6,8].

The mutual information between the past and the future of the sequence is termed its excess entropy:

$$\mathbf{E} = I[\overleftarrow{X}; \overrightarrow{X}]. \tag{1}$$

This quantifies the amount of information from the past of the process that determines its future. For example, $\mathbf{E} = 0$ would mean that the future of the process is independent of the past.

Crutchfield and Young [7] suggested a simple method for modeling a stochastic process that captures the information being communicated from $\overleftarrow{X}$ to $\overrightarrow{X}$: group all the histories that predict the same future. This gives rise to a state machine which they call an ϵ-machine, defined in [8]:

$$\epsilon(\overleftarrow{x}) = \{\overleftarrow{x}' | Pr(\overrightarrow{X} | \overleftarrow{x}) = Pr(\overrightarrow{X} | \overleftarrow{x}')\}. \tag{2}$$

In other words, the states of an ϵ-machine correspond to sets of histories that are equivalent in terms of the probability distributions they assign to the future of the process. ϵ-machines have a number of interesting and useful properties. For instance, causal states are Markovian because $\overleftarrow{X}$ is statistically independent of $\overrightarrow{X}$ given the current causal state of the process. They are also optimally predictive because they capture all of the information in $\overleftarrow{X}$ that is predictive of $\overrightarrow{X}$.

Shalizi and Shalizi have presented an algorithm for learning ϵ-machines from time series data, known as *Causal State Splitting Reconstruction* (CSSR) [19]. CSSR learns a function, η, that is *next-step sufficient* and that can be calculated recursively. A next-step sufficient function is a function that can predict the next step of the time series optimally. If it is also recursively calculable, then it can be used to predict the entire future of the time series optimally.

CSSR learns an ϵ-machine as a Hidden Markov Model (HMM) in an incremental fashion. The HMM is initialized with just one state and, as the algorithm processes the time series, more states are added when a statistical test shows that the current set of states is insufficient for capturing all the information in the past of the time series.

Informally, the CSSR algorithm works as follows. It tests the distribution over the next symbol given increasingly longer past sequences. Let L be the length of the past sequences considered so far, and let Σ be the set of causal states estimated so far.

In the next step, CSSR looks at sequences of length $L + 1$. If a sequence of the form ax^L, where x^L is a sequence of length L and $a \in \mathcal{A}$ is a symbol, belongs to the same causal state as x^L, then we would have [19],

$$Pr(X_t|ax^L) = Pr(X_t|\hat{S} = \hat{\epsilon}(x^L)), \tag{3}$$

where $\hat{S}$ is the current estimate of the causal state to which x^L belongs. This hypothesis can be tested using a statistical test such as the Kolmogorov-Smirnov (KS) test. If the test shows that the LHS and RHS of Eq. 3 are statistically significantly different distributions, then CSSR tries to match the sequence ax^L with all the other causal states estimated so far. If $Pr(X_t|ax^L)$ turns out to be significantly different in all cases, a new causal state is created and ax^L is assigned to it. This process is carried out up to some length L_{max}.

After this, transient states are removed and the state machine is made deterministic by splitting states as necessary. Details of this step can be found in [19] but are not relevant for the present work.

4   Our Approach

Our approach adapts the causal state formalism by treating the trajectory of each agent in the simulation as an instance of the same stochastic process.

In our approach, a multiagent simulation consists of a set of agents, each of which is defined by a k-dimensional state vector $\mathbf{x}(t) = [x_1(t), x_2(t), \ldots x_k(t)]^\mathsf{T}$, which evolves over time. Let d_i be the number of possible values x_i can take. The simulation proceeds in discrete time steps from $t = 0$ to $t = T$. Let the number of agents be denoted by N.

We use the term state in a broad sense. It can include, e.g., the action taken by the agent at each time step. It can also include historical aggregations of variables, e.g., it might include a variable that tracks if an agent has ever done a particular action, or the cumulative value of some variable so far.

Our goal is not to learn an ϵ-machine for a simulation, for two reasons. First, the set of states discovered (e.g., through CSSR), can be hard to interpret. Second, in general, we don't need to predict every step of the simulation. We only care about particular outcomes and the state transitions that are causally-relevant to those outcomes.

Thus, our goal is to compress the trajectory of each agent through state space to a small number of important states that have a significant impact on the outcomes we care about. Let the outcome variable for agent i be denoted by y_i. We assume that y_i is an instance of a random variable Y. Our algorithm for summarization proceeds as follows.

We divide the agent population into a set of clusters, $C(t) = \{C_1(t) \cup C_2(t) \cup \ldots C_m(t)\}$ at each time step. Initially, all the agents are grouped into just one cluster, i.e., $m = 1$ at $t = 0$. At each subsequent time step, the state of each agent changes because one or more of the state variables $(x_1, \ldots x_k)$ changes. The number of ways in which $\mathbf{x}$ can change is $d = d_1 \times d_2 \times \ldots \times d_k$.

Consider an arbitrary cluster of agents, $C_i(t)$. At time step $t + 1$, it can split into up to d groups, based on how each agent's state changes. However, not all of these changes may have a significant impact on the outcome. We treat each group derived from $C_i(t)$ as a candidate cluster, denoted by $CC_{i,j}(t + 1)$, where $j \in 1 \ldots d$. At each step, we compare $Pr(Y|C_i(t))$ with $Pr(Y|CC_{i,j}(t+1))$ using the Kolmogorov-Smirnov (KS) test. Here $Pr(Y|C_i(t))$ is the probability distribution over the final outcomes for all agents that belong to cluster $C_i(t)$ at time step t. If Y is a discrete variable, $Pr(Y = y|C_i(t))$ can be computed as a naive maximum likelihood estimate, i.e., ratio of the number of agents who belong to cluster $C_i(t)$ at time step t and have final outcome $Y = y$ to the number of agents who belong to cluster $C_i(t)$ at time step t. Similarly, $Pr(Y|CC_{i,j}(t+1))$ is the probability distribution over the final outcome for all agents who belong to candidate cluster $CC_{i,j}(t + 1)$ at time step $t + 1$ which is a subset of agents who belong to cluster $C_i(t)$ at time step t and can be computed in a similar fashion. Our null hypothesis (analogous to Eq. 3) is,

$$Pr(Y|CC_{i,j}(t + 1)) = Pr(Y|C_i(t)). \tag{4}$$

We also introduce a parameter δ, which is a threshold on the "effect size", which we measure as the Kullback-Leibler divergence (KL-divergence) between $Pr(Y|C_i(t))$ and $Pr(Y|CC_{i,j}(t+1))$. If the null hypothesis is rejected at a level α (say 0.001) and $D_{KL}(Pr(Y|C_i(t))||Pr(Y|CC_{i,j}(t + 1))) > \delta$, then candidate cluster $CC_{i,j}(t + 1)$ is accepted as a new cluster at time step $t + 1$. The need for the effect size threshold is explained further below. If none of the candidate clusters at time step $t + 1$ are accepted, then $C_i(t)$ is added to the set of clusters for time step $t + 1$.

Thus, the entire simulation is decomposed into a tree structure of agent clusters. Furthermore, each cluster splits only when the corresponding state change is informative about the final outcome of concern.

The trajectory of each agent traces a path through this tree structure. We compress the trajectory by retaining only those time steps at which the cluster to which the agent belongs splits off from its parent cluster. The parameter δ allows us to control how many new clusters are formed at each step, and consequently, how much compression of trajectories we achieve. Setting δ to a high value will retain only the clusters which have a large difference in outcomes from their parent clusters. The summarization algorithm is presented using pseudo-code in Algorithm 1.

Algorithm 1. Simulation Summarization.

input	: $\mathbf{x}_i(t), y_i$, where $i \in 1 \ldots N, t \in 0 \ldots T$
output	: $C(t), t \in 0 \ldots T$: a set of clusters for each time step, organized as a tree over time
parameters	: α: significance level for KS test
	δ: "effect size" threshold on KL-divergence

Initialization: $C(0) \leftarrow$ all agents
for $t \leftarrow 1$ *to* T **do**
   for $i \leftarrow 1$ *to* $|C(t-1)|$ **do**
      Generate $CC(t)$, the set of candidate clusters for time step t
      for $j \leftarrow 1$ *to* d **do**
         Test the null hypothesis (Eqn. 4) for each candidate cluster and its parent.
         if *null hypothesis is rejected at level* α *and*
         $D_{KL}(Pr(Y|C_i(t))||Pr(Y|CC_{i,j}(t+1))) > \delta$ **then**
            $C(t) \leftarrow CC_{i,j}(t)$

The set of compressed agent trajectories ultimately constitutes our summary representation of the simulation. It can be queried for various quantities of interest, as will be illustrated in the experiments in the next sections.

It may happen that the agent state in the simulation is described by a large number of variables. For example, in our experiments with the large-scale disaster simulation, agent state is defined by about 40 variables which could take binary, categorical or continuous values, leading to a very large state space. Large state space would make the algorithm computationally expensive. In this case, one can select a subset of state variables to be included in the k-dimensional state vector. However, the decision about which state variables are included in the k-dimensional state vector generally requires some domain knowledge about the underlying process. Results of the summarization algorithm would also depend upon this selection.

5   Experiments with a Toy Domain

In this section we present results from a couple of toy examples to illustrate how our algorithm works.

5.1   Example 1

Here, we present results from a toy example where a set of agents do a random walk on a 5-by-5 grid. There are 100K agents and all of them start at the same location (2, 2) on the grid. At each time step, they move to a neighboring cell (including staying at the same cell) at random. An agent gets a reward when it reaches cell (5, 5). For simplicity, once an agent gets a reward, it does not move.

The condition under which agents obtain reward is unknown to them. Please note that we are not actually learning a policy to maximize the reward. It is just a simple process to illustrate the functioning of our algorithm.

We run this simulation for 30 iterations and about 26500 agents got rewards at the end of the simulation. The state vector for each agent consists of its X and Y coordinates. We tried two different values of KL-divergence threshold, δ: 0.3 and 0.5.

Figures 1a–c show a sample trajectory and corresponding compressed trajectories for δ values 0.3 and 0.5, respectively. The high value of δ (0.5) can only identify states that cause sudden changes in probability distribution over final outcomes and hence identifies cell (5, 5) as the causal state. While the lower δ (0.3) can detect gradual changes and hence identifies neighbors of cell (5, 5) also as once an agent reaches cell (5, 4), it is easy to reach cell (5, 5).

Figure 2 shows the number of clusters vs. iteration for different threshold values. As small values of δ can detect gradual changes, while higher values of δ can only detect bigger changes, the number of clusters decreases as δ increases. Please note that the minimum size of a cluster is constrained to be 30 (so that the number of samples in a cluster are enough for performing a statistical test) and this poses a limit on splitting and hence identifying states that do not appear enough number of times.

Table 1. Compression

δ	Compression
0.3	0.051
0.5	0.0333

Overall compression defined as ratio of average length of compressed trajectory to length of uncompressed trajectory is as shown in Table 1. As expected, higher value of δ leads to higher compression. It also captures the most relevant state (5, 5) (Fig. 3). Figure 3 shows the number of times a given cell appears in a compressed trajectory for $\delta = 0.5$. Other cells appear in compressed trajectories only in later iterations. These are the cells from which an agent can not reach cell (5, 5) by iteration 30. So the values of state variables (cell here) along with the reward probability give information about state-reward structure.

5.2   Example 2

In this example, agents move around on a 10-by-10 grid which is divided into four rooms, each of size 5-by-5 as shown in Fig. 4. Each room has two doors leading to neighboring rooms. There are 500K agents and all of them start at cell (1, 1)

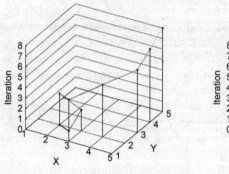 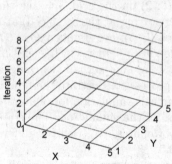

(a) Original trajectory   (b) Compressed trajectory for $\delta = 0.3$

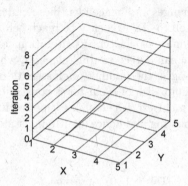

(c) Compressed trajectory for $\delta = 0.5$

Fig. 1. A sample trajectory at various levels of compression.

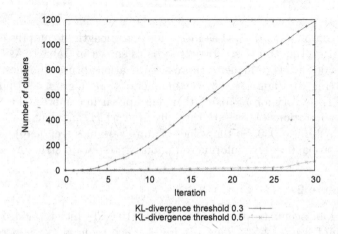

Fig. 2. Number of clusters vs. iteration for toy example 1

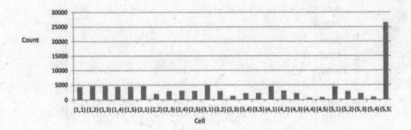

Fig. 3. Frequency distribution for cells in compressed trajectories.

and an agent gets a reward when it reaches cell (10, 10). For simplicity, once an agent reaches the reward location, it stays there till the end of the simulation. At each step, with a small bias (probability 0.3), an agent tries to move towards the reward location (i.e., agents in the lower-left room move towards the nearest door, agents in lower-right and upper-left rooms move towards the door leading to the upper-right room, and agents in the upper-right room move towards the reward location (10, 10)) and with the rest of the probability, it moves to a neighboring cell (including staying at the same cell) at random.

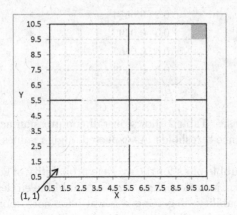

Fig. 4. Toy example 2 consisting of four rooms where each room has two doors leading to the neighboring rooms. All agents start at cell (1, 1) and an agent gets a reward when it reaches cell (10, 10). In order to reach a reward location, each agent has to pass through at least two doors.

We run this simulation for 30 iterations and 112580 agents got rewards at the end of the simulation. The state vector for each agent consists of its X and Y coordinates. We tried five values of KL-divergence threshold, δ: 0.1, 0.2, 0.3, 0.4, and 0.5. Figure 5 shows the number of clusters vs. iteration for different threshold values. Similar to the previous example, as small values of δ can detect gradual changes while the high values of δ can only detect bigger changes in the probability distribution over the final outcomes, the number of clusters

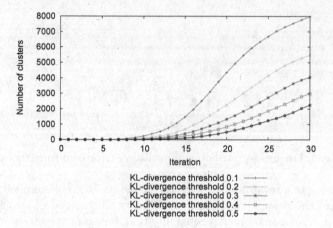

Fig. 5. Number of clusters vs. iteration for toy example 2.

Table 2. Compression

δ	Compression
0.1	0.0664
0.2	0.0554
0.3	0.0499
0.4	0.0463
0.5	0.0438

decreases as δ increases. Table 2 shows overall compression achieved for various values of KL-divergence thresholds. As expected, higher values of δ lead to higher compression.

Figure 6 shows bubble plots for the average probability of getting a reward for cells in compressed trajectories. Here, sizes of solid blue circles are proportional to the average probability of getting a reward for corresponding cells in the compressed trajectories for all agents and across all iterations and hollow black circles show cells that do not appear in any compressed trajectory. As high values of KL-divergence threshold (i.e., $\delta = 0.5$; Fig. 6c) can only identify cells that lead to higher changes in the probability of getting a reward, it identifies cells in the upper-right room (where the reward locations and it's neighboring cells have high probability of getting a reward) and some cells in upper-left and lower-right rooms (near doors leading to the upper-right room). It also identifies some cells in the lower-left room though the probability of getting reward for these cells is quite low. It also misses doors in the lower-left room that lead to the neighboring rooms. An intermediate value of $\delta = 0.3$ (Fig. 6b) can identify more cells including those leading to doors in the lower-left room. Finally a lower value of $\delta = 0.1$ (Fig. 6a) identifies all cells and further, for most of the cells, the probabilities of reward are proportional to their distances from the reward

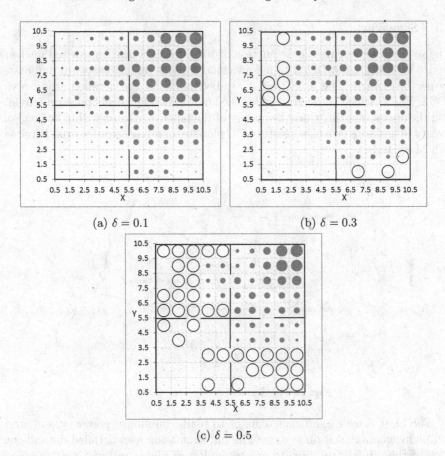

(a) $\delta = 0.1$ (b) $\delta = 0.3$

(c) $\delta = 0.5$

Fig. 6. Bubble plots for the average probability of getting a reward for cells in compressed trajectories. Here, sizes of solid blue circles are proportional to the average probability of getting a reward for corresponding cells in the compressed trajectories for all agents and across all iterations and hollow black circles show cells that do not appear in any compressed trajectory. (Color figure online)

location. This information is similar to what one would expect from calculating state-value functions and provides information about the optimal policy, to move (from the current cell) to the neighboring cell with the highest probability of reward.

6   Large-Scale Disaster Simulation

Now, we turn to a very complex multiagent simulation of a human-initiated disaster scenario. Our simulation consists of a large, detailed "synthetic population" [3] of agents, and also includes detailed infrastructure models. We briefly describe this simulation below before summarizing the results from it using our algorithm.

6.1 Scenario

The scenario represents the detonation of 10kT hypothetical improvised nuclear device in Washington DC. The fallout cloud spreads mainly eastward and east-by-northeastward. The area that is studied is called the detailed study area (DSA; Fig. 7) which is the area under the largest thermal effects polygon (circle) and the area under the widest boundary of the fallout contours within DC region county boundaries (which consists of DC plus surrounding counties from Virginia and Maryland).

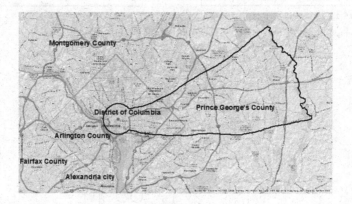

Fig. 7. The detailed study area (DSA).

The blast causes significant damage to roads, buildings, power system, and cell phone communication system. The full simulation uses detailed data about each of these infrastructures to create models of phone call and text message capacity [5], altered movement patterns due to road damage [1], injuries due to rubble and debris, and levels of radiation protection in damaged buildings.

6.2 Agent Design and Behavior

The scenario affects all people present in DSA at the time of detonation which includes area residents, transients (tourists and business travelers), and dorm students. Health and behavior of an individual depends upon its demographics as well as its location in the immediate aftermath of the event. This information is obtained from synthetic population [2]. Synthetic population is an agent-based representation of a population of a region along with their demographic (e.g., age, income, family structure) and activity related information (e.g., type of activity, location, start time). Detailed description about creating residents, transients, and dorm students can be found in [2,14,15]. There are 730,833 people present in DSA at the time of detonation which is the same as the number of agents in the simulation.

Apart from demographics and location (as obtained from synthetic population), agents are defined by a number of other variables like health (modeled on a 0 to 7 range where 0 is dead and 7 corresponds to full health), behavior (described in the next paragraph), whether the agent is out of the affected area, whether the agent is the group leader, whether the agent has received emergency broadcast (EBR), the agent's exposure to radiation, etc.

Each agent keeps track of family members' health states which could be unknown, known to be healthy, or known to be injured. This knowledge is updated whenever it makes a successful call to a family member or meets them in person.

Follow-the-leader behavior is also modeled, i.e., once family members encounter each other, they move together from there on. One of them becomes the group leader and others follow him. This kind of behavior is well-documented in emergency situations. Similarly when a person is rescued by someone, that person travels with the rescuer until he reaches a hospital or meets his family members.

Agent behavior is conceptually based on the formalism of decentralized semi-Markov decision process (Dec-SMDP) with communication [10] using the framework of options [20]. Here, high level behaviors are modeled as options, which are policies with initiation and termination conditions. Agents can choose among six options: household reconstitution (HRO), evacuation, shelter-seeking (Shelter), healthcare-seeking (HC-seeking), panic, and aid & assist. High level behavior options correspond to low level action plans which model their dependency with infrastructural systems. These actions are: call, text or move. Whom to call or text and where to move depends upon the current behavior option, e.g., in household reconstitution option, a person tries to move towards a family member and/or call family members while in healthcare-seeking option, a person tries to call 911 or to move towards a hospital. Details of the behavior model can be found in [14].

6.3 Experiments

Our goal here is to generate a summary for the disaster simulation. Agents and locations that they visit are represented by about 40 variables which could take binary, categorical or continuous values, leading to a very large state space. Hence, here we focus on subsets of these variables for generating summary.

We use data for the first 30 iterations and use the probability distribution over the final health state (in iteration 100, 48 h after the blast) to identify causal states that affect the final health state.

Effect of Behavior and Emergency Broadcast

In first experiment, we only use two variables to split clusters: if received emergency broadcast (EBR, 1 if received and 0 otherwise) and behavior. Here, apart from the six behavior options mentioned in the previous section, behavior variable also includes two categories indicating if an agent is in healthcare location (in HC loc) and if it is out of area.

We try three different values of δ: 1, 2, and 5. Figure 8 shows number of clusters for different values of threshold. As higher values of δ can only identify

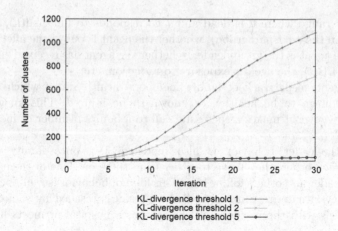

Fig. 8. Number of clusters when considering EBR and behavior only.

sudden changes in the outcomes, $\delta = 5$ only identifies changes when agents die. We compare the causal states identified by other two threshold values next.

We save the compressed trajectories in a database table along with the expected value of final health state. This table can be used to query any subpopulation for the outcome of interest. For example, identify transitions by iteration 6 (within first hour) where the expected final health state is improved, order by expected improvement in descending order. Top results for $\delta = 2$ and $\delta = 1$ are shown in Tables 3 and 4, respectively.

Table 3. Effect of EBR and behavior, $\delta = 2$

Rank	Iteration	EBR	Behavior
1	2	0	Out of area
2	3	0	Out of area
3	5	0	In HC loc
4	6	0	In HC loc

Here, $\delta = 2$ shows that being at healthcare location and out of area are important for improving health outcomes. As expected, $\delta = 1$ shows more gradual transitions and shows that evacuation is also important from health perspective. It is evacuation behavior that leads to out of area.

Effects of More Variables

Here, apart from EBR and behavior, we also include current health state, radiation exposure level (with four levels: low, medium, high, and very high), if received treatment, and distance from ground zero (with three levels (based on

Table 4. Effect of EBR and behavior, $\delta = 1$

Rank	Iteration	EBR	Behavior
1	2	0	Out of area
2	3	0	Out of area
3	6	0	In HC loc
4	4	1	Out of area
5	4	1	In HC loc
6	3	0	Evacuation
7	4	0	Out of area
8	2	0	Evacuation
9	5	0	In HC loc

damage zones as described in [4]): less than 0.6 miles, between 0.6 and 1 mile, and greater than 1 mile). We set $\delta = 5$ and evaluate six queries as below:

Query 1: Identify top 10 transitions by iteration 10 where current health state remains the same (so improvement is not due to current health state) but the expected final health state is improved, order by expected improvement in descending order. Top results are shown in Table 5.

Table 5. Top results for query 1.

Rank	Iteration	Health state	EBR	Behavior	Radiation exposure	Treatment	Distance from ground zero
1	8	5	0	In HC loc	High	0	>0.6 mile, <1 mile
2	8	7	1	Panic	Medium	0	>1 mile
3	10	5	0	Out of area	Medium	0	>1 mile
4	9	6	0	Out of area	Medium	0	>1 mile
5	4	4	0	In HC loc	High	0	>0.6 mile, <1 mile
6	7	7	0	Out of area	Medium	0	>1 mile
7	3	4	0	In HC loc	High	0	>0.6 mile, <1 mile
8	8	7	0	Out of area	Medium	0	>1 mile
9	8	6	0	Out of area	Medium	0	>1 mile
10	9	7	0	Out of area	Medium	0	>1 mile

Results show that for agents who are within 1 mile of ground zero, are in health state 4 or 5, reaching healthcare location by iteration 10 helps improving health, even if the exposure level is high. Here, the value of treatment variable is zero which means that these agents have reached healthcare location but have not yet received treatment. This suggests that atleast initially (within first 3 h) there are not long queues at these healthcare locations and so once an agent reaches healthcare location, it is quite likely that it will receive treatment which leads to an improved health. For agents in healthstate 5 to 7, who are far from ground zero though with medium exposure, getting out of area helps. Also, for agents in health state 7, who are far from ground zero, with medium exposure, and panicking, receiving EBR helps (as it provides information about the event and recommends sheltering).

Please note that the algorithm only finds states that affect the final outcomes significantly. Interpretation of the results requires some domain knowledge. For example, it is our knowledge that suggest that reaching healthcare location helps even if the exposure to radiation is high, not receiving high radiation exposure at healthcare location.

Next we identify states that reduce the expected health state by iteration 10.

Query 2: Identify top 10 transitions by iteration 10 where current health state remains the same (so reduction is not due to current health state) but the expected final health state is reduced, order by expected reduction in descending order. Top results are shown in Table 6.

Table 6. Top results for query 2.

Rank	Iteration	Health state	EBR	Behavior	Radiation exposure	Treatment	Distance from ground zero
1	10	3	0	HC-seeking	Low	0	>1 mile
2	9	3	0	HC-seeking	Low	0	>1 mile
3	7	7	0	HRO	High	0	<0.6 mile
4	5	3	0	Panic	Low	0	>1 mile
5	5	3	0	HC-seeking	Low	0	>1 mile
6	4	3	0	HC-seeking	Low	0	>1 mile
7	9	7	0	HRO	High	0	<0.6 mile
8	8	7	0	HRO	High	0	<0.6 mile
9	4	3	0	Panic	High	0	>1 mile
10	7	3	0	Panic	High	0	>1 mile

For agents who are currently in a full health, close to ground zero, and have high exposure level, doing household reconstitution (HRO) reduces their expected outcome. Even if the current health state is good, this accounts for the delayed effect of radiation. For people who are already in low health (health state 3), panicking or seeking healthcare (which makes them travel to healthcare location and exposed to more radiation) deteriorates expected health state, even if far from ground zero.

For people who are close to ground zero (within 0.6 mile from ground zero which is a severe damage zone [4]), the likelihood of survival is very low while for people who are further than 1 mile (in light damage zone [4]), though they may have minor injuries, they can survive by themselves. However, survival is more complicated between 0.6 to 1 mile (defined as moderate damage zone) and hence next we run queries to see what people who started between 0.6 to 1 mile did that improved or reduced their expected final health.

Query 3: For people who started between 0.6 and 1 mile, identify top 10 transitions where current health state remains the same and current distance is less than 1 mile (so improvement is not due to current health state or current distance) but the expected final health state is improved, order by expected improvement in descending order. Top results are shown in Table 7.

Table 7. Top results for query 3.

Rank	Iteration	Health state	EBR	Behavior	Radiation exposure	Treatment	Distance from ground zero
1	29	5	0	Shelter	Medium	0	>0.6 mile, <1 mile
2	24	5	0	Shelter	Medium	0	>0.6 mile, <1 mile
3	25	5	0	Shelter	Medium	0	>0.6 mile, <1 mile
4	4	4	0	In HC loc	High	0	>0.6 mile, <1 mile
5	21	6	0	Shelter	Low	1	>0.6 mile, <1 mile
6	3	4	0	In HC loc	High	0	>0.6 mile, <1 mile
7	14	5	0	Shelter	Medium	0	>0.6 mile, <1 mile
8	23	5	0	Shelter	Medium	0	>0.6 mile, <1 mile
9	4	5	0	In HC loc	Low	0	>0.6 mile, <1 mile
10	3	5	0	In HC loc	Medium	0	>0.6 mile, <1 mile

Results show that for people who started between 0.6 and 1 mile, reaching healthcare location early on (within first hour) helps improving expected final health, even if moderately injured (health state 4) and have high radiation exposure. For people with minor injury (health state 5) and with medium exposure to radiation, sheltering later on helps. Please not that even though our algorithm suggests so, it is not just sheltering in these particular iterations (14, 23, 24, 25 or 29) that helps but it is sheltering for a long period prior to and upto these iterations which improves expected health. This is because currently our algorithm does not detect effects of a sequence of particular actions (e.g., sheltering for a long period of time) and we would like to adapt it in the future for detecting effects of sequential actions.

Query 4: For people who started between 0.6 and 1 mile, identify top 10 transitions where current health state remains the same (so reduction is not due to current health state) but the expected final health state is reduced, order by expected reduction in descending order. Top results are shown in Table 8.

For people who started between 0.6 and 1 mile, who are currently in full health (health state 7) and with medium radiation exposure, household reconstitution and aid & assist reduces their expected final health. While for people who are already in low health (health state 3), though with low radiation exposure, panicking or seeking healthcare reduces health. This is because these behaviors

Table 8. Top results for query 4.

Rank	Iteration	Health state	EBR	Behavior	Radiation exposure	Treatment	Distance from ground zero
1	9	3	0	HC-seeking	Low	0	>1 mile
2	7	7	0	HRO	High	0	<0.6 mile
3	17	7	0	Aid & Assist	High	0	<0.6 mile
4	12	3	0	HC-seeking	Low	0	>1 mile
5	4	3	0	HC-seeking	Low	0	>1 mile
6	9	7	0	HRO	High	0	<0.6 mile
7	8	7	0	HRO	High	0	<0.6 mile
8	4	3	0	Panic	Low	0	>1 mile
9	5	7	0	HRO	High	0	>0.6 mile, <1 mile
10	3	3	0	HC-seeking	Low	0	>1 mile

make them go outside looking for information, family members, other injured people, or nearest healthcare locations, exposing them to further radiation.

One of the major concerns in a nuclear blast scenario is exposure to radiation. So next we look at what transitions improves expected final health even if the radiation exposure is high.

Query 5: For people with high radiation exposure, identify top 10 transitions where current health state remains the same (so improvement is not due to current health state) but the expected final health state is improved, order by expected improvement in descending order. Top results are shown in Table 9.

Table 9. Top results for query 5.

Rank	Iteration	Health state	EBR	Behavior	Radiation exposure	Treatment	Distance from ground zero
1	8	5	0	In HC loc	High	0	>0.6 mile, <1 mile
2	4	4	0	In HC loc	High	0	>0.6 mile, <1 mile
3	29	7	1	Out of area	High	0	>1 mile
4	3	4	0	In HC loc	High	0	>0.6 mile, <1 mile
5	14	3	0	Out of area	High	0	>1 mile
6	16	7	0	HRO	High	0	>1 mile
7	19	7	1	Out of area	High	0	>1 mile
8	10	3	0	HC-seeking	High	0	>0.6 mile, <1 mile
9	25	3	1	HC-seeking	High	0	>0.6 mile, <1 mile
10	18	7	0	Out of area	High	0	>1 mile

Results show that for people with already high radiation exposure and minor or severe injuries (i.e., health state between 3 to 5), seeking healthcare or reaching healthcare location helps even if close to ground zero (i.e., distance is less than 1 mile). For people in full health and far from ground zero, household reconstitution or getting out of area helps. Here, benefits of household reconstitution seem counter-intuitive as it makes people go outside looking for family members and hence exposed to radiation. But further analysis show that household reconstitution leads about 80% of these people out of the affected area by iteration 50.

At last, let's look at transitions that worsen the expected final health even if radiation exposure is low and have minor or less injuries (health state ≥ 5).

Query 6: For people with low radiation exposure and minor or less injuries (i.e., health state ≥ 5), identify top 10 transitions where current health state remains the same (so reduction is not due to current health state) but the expected final health state is reduced, order by expected reduction in descending order. Top results are shown in Table 10.

Table 10. Top results for query 6.

Rank	Iteration	Health state	EBR	Behavior	Radiation exposure	Treatment	Distance from ground zero
1	6	5	0	HC-seeking	Low	0	>0.6 mile, <1 mile
2	6	5	0	Panic	Low	0	>0.6 mile, <1 mile
3	11	5	1	HC-seeking	Low	0	>1 mile
4	3	5	0	HC-seeking	Low	0	>0.6 mile, <1 mile
5	11	5	0	HC-seeking	Low	0	>0.6 mile, <1 mile
6	24	5	0	HC-seeking	Low	0	>1 mile
7	5	5	0	Shelter	Low	0	>0.6 mile, <1 mile
8	6	5	0	HRO	Low	0	>0.6 mile, <1 mile
9	29	5	0	Out of area	Low	0	>1 mile
10	16	5	0	HC-seeking	Low	0	>1 mile

Results show that for people with low radiation exposure and minor injuries (i.e., health state 5), household reconstitution, panic, and seeking healthcare reduces expected final health even if far from ground zero as these behaviors lead them outside looking for family members, information or healthcare and expose to radiation.

We see, in the above queries, that a number of meaningful states have been discovered by the summary.

7   Conclusion

As large-scale and complex simulations are becoming common, there is a need for methods to effectively summarize results from a simulation run. Here, we present a simulation summarization as a problem of extracting causal states (including actions) from agents' trajectories. We present an algorithm that identifies states that change the probability distributions over final outcomes. Such causal states compress agent trajectories in such a way that only states that change the distribution of final outcomes significantly are extracted.

These extracted trajectories can be stored in a database and queried. A threshold on effect size is used to specify what change is considered significant. Higher value of this threshold identify states that cause sudden changes in final outcomes while smaller values can identify gradual changes.

We present a toy example to show the effectiveness of our algorithm and then apply it to a large-scale simulation of the aftermath of a disaster in a major urban area. It identifies being in a healthcare location, sheltering, evacuation, and being out of the area as states that improve health outcomes while panic, household reconstitution, and healthcare-seeking as states (behaviors) that worsen health.

There are several directions for future work. Summary representations can be used to compare simulations with different parameter settings to identify if parameter changes result in changes in causal mechanisms. Summary representations can potentially also be used for anomaly detection.

Acknowledgments. We thank our external collaborators and members of the Network Dynamics and Simulation Science Lab (NDSSL) for their suggestions and comments. This work has been supported in part by DTRA CNIMS Contract HDTRA1-11-D-0016-0001, DTRA Grant HDTRA1-11-1-0016, NIH MIDAS Grant 5U01GM070694-11, NIH Grant 1R01GM109718, NSF NetSE Grant CNS-1011769, and NSF SDCI Grant OCI-1032677.

References

1. Adiga, A., Mortveit, H.S., Wu, S.: Route stability in large-scale transportation models. In: MAIN: The Workshop on Multiagent Interaction Networks at AAMAS 2013, Saint Paul, Minnesota, USA (2013)
2. Barrett, C., Beckman, R., Berkbigler, K., Bisset, K., Bush, B., Campbell, K., Eubank, S., Henson, K., Hurford, J., Kubicek, D., Marathe, M., Romero, P., Smith, J., Smith, L., Speckman, P., Stretz, P., Thayer, G., Eeckhout, E., Williams, M.D.: TRANSIMS: transportation analysis simulation system. Technical report LA-UR-00-1725. An earlier version appears as a 7 part technical report series LA-UR-99-1658 and LA-UR-99-2574 to LA-UR-99-2580, Los Alamos National Laboratory Unclassified Report (2001)
3. Barrett, C., Eubank, S., Marathe, A., Marathe, M., Swarup, S.: Synthetic information environments for policy informatics: a distributed cognition perspective. In: Johnston, E. (ed.) Governance in the Information Era: Theory and Practice of Policy Informatics, pp. 267–284. Routledge, New York (2015)
4. Buddemeier, B.R., Valentine, J.E., Millage, K.K., Brandt, L.D., Region, N.C.: Key response planning factors for the aftermath of nuclear terrorism. Technical report LLNL-TR-512111, Lawrence Livermore National Lab, November 2011
5. Chandan, S., Saha, S., Barrett, C., Eubank, S., Marathe, A., Marathe, M., Swarup, S., Vullikanti, A.K.S.: Modeling the interaction between emergency communications and behavior in the aftermath of a disaster. In: Greenberg, A.M., Kennedy, W.G., Bos, N.D. (eds.) SBP 2013. LNCS, vol. 7812, pp. 476–485. Springer, Heidelberg (2013). doi:10.1007/978-3-642-37210-0_52
6. Crutchfield, J.P., Ellison, C.J., Mahoney, J.R.: Time's barbed arrow: irreversibility, crypticity, and stored information. Phys. Rev. Lett. **103**(9), 094101 (2009)

7. Crutchfield, J.P., Young, K.: Inferring statistical complexity. Phys. Rev. Lett. **63**(2), 105–108 (1989)
8. Ellison, C.J., Mahoney, J.R., Crutchfield, J.P.: Prediction, retrodiction, and the amount of information stored in the present. J. Stat. Phys. **136**(6), 1005–1034 (2009)
9. Ferguson, N.M., Cummings, D.A.T., Cauchemez, S., Fraser, C., Riley, S., Meeyai, A., Iamsirithaworn, S., Burke, D.S.: Strategies for containing an emerging influenza pandemic in Southeast Asia. Nature **437**, 209–214 (2005)
10. Goldman, C.V., Zilberstein, S.: Communication-based decomposition mechanisms for decentralized MDPs. J. Artif. Int. Res. **32**(1), 169–202 (2008)
11. Marshall, B.D.L., Galea, S.: Formalizing the role of agent-based modeling in causal inference and epidemiology. Am. J. Epidemiol. **181**(2), 92–99 (2015)
12. Meliou, A., Gatterbauer, W., Halpern, J.Y., Koch, C., Moore, K.F., Suciu, D.: Causality in databases. IEEE Data Eng. Bull. **33**(3), 59–67 (2010)
13. Meliou, A., Gatterbauer, W., Moore, K.F., Suciu, D.: Why so? or why no? functional causality for explaining query answers. In: Proceedings of the 4th International Workshop on Management of Uncertain Data (MUD), pp. 3–17 (2010)
14. Parikh, N., Swarup, S., Stretz, P.E., Rivers, C.M., Lewis, B.L., Marathe, M.V., Eubank, S.G., Barrett, C.L., Lum, K., Chungbaek, Y.: Modeling human behavior in the aftermath of a hypothetical improvised nuclear detonation. In: Proceedings of the International Conference on Autonomous Agents and Multiagent Systems (AAMAS), Saint Paul, MN, USA, May 2013
15. N. Parikh, M. Youssef, S. Swarup, and S. Eubank. Modeling the effect of transient populations on epidemics in Washington DC. Sci Rep. **3** (2013). Article No. 3152
16. Shahaf, D., Guestrin, C., Horvitz, E.: Metro maps of science. In: Proceedings of KDD (2012)
17. Shahaf, D., Guestrin, C., Horvitz, E.: Trains of thought: generating information maps. In: Proceedings of WWW, Lyon, France (2012)
18. Shalizi, C.R., Crutchfield, J.P.: Computational mechanics: pattern and prediction, structure and simplicity. J. Stat. Phys. **104**(3/4), 817–879 (2001)
19. Shalizi, C.R., Shalizi, K.L.: Blind construction of optimal nonlinear recursive predictors for discrete sequences. In: Chickering, M., Halpern, J. (eds.) Proceedings of the Twentieth Conference on Uncertainty in Artificial Intelligence, Banff, Canada, pp. 504–511 (2004)
20. Sutton, R., Precup, D., Singh, S.: Between MDPs and semi-MDPs: a framework for temporal abstraction in reinforcement learning. Artif. Intell. **112**(1–2), 181–211 (1999)
21. Ver Steeg, G. Galstyan, A.: Information transfer in social media. In: Proceedings of WWW (2012)
22. Walloth, C., Gurr, J.M., Schmidt, J.A. (eds.): Understanding Complex Urban Systems: Multidisciplinary Approaches to Modeling. Springer, Cham (2014). doi:10.1007/978-3-319-02996-2
23. Wein, L.M., Choi, Y., Denuit, S.: Analyzing evacuation versus shelter-in-place strategies after a terrorist nuclear detonation. Risk Anal. **30**(6), 1315–1327 (2010)

MABS Applications

To Big Wing, or Not to Big Wing, Now an Answer

Matthew Oldham[✉]

Department of Computational and Data Sciences, Computational Social Science
Program, George Mason University, 4400 University Drive, Fairfax, VA 22030, USA
moldham@gmu.edu

Abstract. The Churchilliaṛ quote "Never, in the field of human conflict,
was so much owed by so many to so few" [3], encapsulates perfectly the
heroics of Royal Air Force (RAF) Fighter Command (FC) during the
Battle of Britain. Despite the undoubted heroics, questions remain about
how FC employed the 'so few'. In particular, the question as to whether
FC should have employed the 'Big Wing' tactics, as per 12 Group, or
implement the smaller wings as per 11 Group, remains a source of much
debate. In this paper, I create an agent based model (ABM) simulation
of the Battle of Britain, which provides valuable insight into the key
components that influenced the loss rates of both sides. It provides mixed
support for the tactics employed by 11 Group, as the model identified
numerous variables that impacted the success or otherwise of the British.

1 Introduction

1.1 The Battle of Britain

The air war that raged over Britain between the 10th of July and 31st of October
1940 is colloquially known as the Battle of Britain. The battle's significance
comes from the fact that not only did the Germans fail to achieve either of their
objectives, but it is seen as the first major campaign to be fought entirely by air
forces [2]. The initial phase of the battle revolved around the German's attempt
to gain air superiority prior to their planned invasion of England – Operation Sea
Lion. After September 6th, the Germans shifted to bombing civilian targets, a
period that has become known as the 'Blitz', as they attempted to force Britain
into surrender.

At the commencement of the battle, the RAF was at a numerical disadvantage having only 754 front line fighters spread across the entire country to combat the combined Luftwaffe force of 2,288 (1,029 fighters and 1,259 bombers) [2].
Despite this numerical disadvantage, the RAF managed to match or exceed the
daily sortie rate of the Luftwaffe [5], achieved with some pilots flying up to four

---

This paper is being reused and has already appeared in Oldham M. (2016) To
Big Wing, or Not to Big Wing, Now an Answer. In: Osman N., Sierra C. (eds.)
Autonomous Agents and Multiagent Systems. AAMAS 2016. Lecture Notes in Com-
puter Science, vol. 10002. Springer, Cham.

© Springer International Publishing AG 2017
L.G. Nardin and L. Antunes (Eds.): MABS 2016, LNAI 10399, pp. 95–110, 2017.
DOI: 10.1007/978-3-319-67477-3_5

sorties a day. The cost of the battle was high for both sides, with FC losing over 1,000 aircraft and 544 of the approximate 3,000 aircrew that participated. Luftwaffe losses totaled nearly 1,900 aircraft and more than 2,600 of their airmen killed [2].

Prior to World War II (WWII) the RAF developed its fighter defense strategy in line with the principles of concentration [7], which stemmed from the Lanchester equation [6] of aimed fire. When it came time to defend Britain, there were two implementations of the FC doctrine. Air Vice Marshall Keith Park, who controlled 11 Group, the Group which bore the brunt of the action in the Battle of Britain, tended to send single or pairs of squadrons (12 aircraft per squadron) to intercept the enemy. This allowed Park to confront the enemy while denying the Luftwaffe a major engagement. Air Vice Marshall Leigh-Mallory who controlled 12 Group, which was typically held in reserve, preferred to form a 'Big Wing' of 5 or more squadrons before engaging [7]. The main issue with this tactic was the time it took to arrange the 'Big Wing', which in turn limited the time the wing had to search for the enemy, and ultimately engage it. Another negative of the tactic for the RAF was that a larger formation was what the Luftwaffe was seeking, as it improved its chances of inflicting greater losses [5].

1.2 The Lanchester Model

The advent of air warfare during the First World War (WWI) necessitated a rethink of existing military doctrine. One such attempt was provided in [6], where Lanchester developed a mathematical model addressing the implications of various combat scenarios, including directed fire. Equation 1 illustrates the general form of the model, where a force's loss rate $\left(\frac{dB}{dt} \ or \ \frac{dG}{dt}\right)$ is dependent on $g(b)$, the kill rate/effectiveness of the opposition, the strengthen of the opposition as given by $G(B)$, raised to a particular power $g1(b2)$, and the strengthen of your force $B(G)$, raised to a particular power $b1(g2)^1$.

$$\frac{dB}{dt} = -gG^{g1}B^{b1}, \qquad \frac{dG}{dt} = -bG^{b2}G^{g2}. \qquad (1)$$

One particular form of the model is the aimed fire model, where $b1 = g2 = 1$ and $b1 = g2 = 0$. These values allow Eq. 1 to be simplified and after setting the conditions by which both forces suffer the same proportional losses $\left(\frac{dB}{dt}\right)/B = \left(\frac{dG}{dt}\right)/G$, the following equation is derived:

$$gG^2 = bB^2. \qquad (2)$$

The importance of Eq. 2 is that when forces are using aimed fire; their fighting strength becomes proportional to a weapon's effectiveness multiplied by the square of the number of weapons employed. The implication being, the concentration of force becomes a vital consideration in military strategy [5].

---

[1] [5] make the point that the $g1$, $b1$, $g2$ and $b2$ have no justification and are used solely to facilitate modeling.

An analysis of the Battle of Britain utilizing the Lanchester model was undertaken by [5] in an attempt to understand whether the 'Big Wing' approach was the correct approach. The conclusion of [5] was that the model was right about British losses, a large German force meant greater losses, but not about German losses. Therefore, the 'Big Wing' appeared to fail as massed battles weakly favored the Germans [5].

1.3   Agent Based Models

The evidence provided by [5] in support of the strategy employed by Park and 11 Group came from fitting the actual daily data from the Battle of Britain to the Lanchester model via regression analysis. While this provided insight in terms of the relevance of the Lanchester model, the results do not provide insight into the dynamics that produced the result. In particular, there is no insight into how Park achieved the 'defender's advantage'. A source of this problem, as [5] points out, is that "the Lanchester models are spatially and temporally homogenous, allowing for no variation in unit type, terrain or tactics, command or control, skill or doctrine". These assumptions appear inconsistent with modern warfare, which is ultimately dynamic and heterogeneous.

The approach utilized by [5] saw the force size estimated by the number of sorties flown by each side on a particular day. [5] indicates that ideally the data would be per raid. However, this was not possible due to the lack of records[2]. While the data shows the proportional loss rate of both sides, importantly it does not convene the loss rate per battle contact, as many sorties did not engage the enemy for a variety of reasons. Therefore, the true performance of the RAF against the Luftwaffe is lost.

An alternate approach is to implement an ABM that is capable of creating a virtual Battle of Britain. The model can be designed to explore the various tactics, and in particular whether the tactics of Park were indeed more effective than those of Leigh-Mallory. ABMs allow for the interaction of individual agents (aircraft/pilots in the proposed model), who undertake actions based on the context of their environment using basic rules. [4] successfully demonstrated the ability of an ABM to analyze air combat by creating a model of the Falklands War air battle. The model produced results consistent with what was observed in the conflict and tested various scenarios by varying the capabilities of both the U.K. and Argentinean forces.

For this paper certain abstractions were made to ensure that the research questions could be addressed in a timely manner. To achieve this, agents perform simplified actions that are supportable by fact or theory. The justification for the abstractions is that the aim of the model was to better understand the consequences of changing the number of squadrons per wing while removing noise from other factors. While this approach may not be fully authentic, it is

---

[2] While [5] were able to provide supporting evidence that binning data by day rather than raid did not invalidate the approach, this author feels an alternative approach is warranted.

more realistic than the Lanchester model and further iterations of the model can enhance the level of authenticity.

The level of abstraction means the model is not a one for one simulation, with a tick accounting for approximately 30 s. Determining the actions of each plane within a 30 s window is all but impossible, hence the simplifications and assumptions. Other abstractions include the weather having no impact, there being a 100% chance of the RAF making contact with an incoming raid[3], and the dogfight algorithm being simplified with concepts such as the role of a wingman removed.

The level of abstraction and available data did present a problem in terms of calibrating the model. Using the data from [5], the Luftwaffe and RAF losses and the number of sorties for each day are known. However, the actual loss rates per combat interactions are not known, which is what the model is actually simulating. An alternate approach was to review the diaries of the individual RAF squadrons. However, these tended to overstate the success rate of the pilots.

2   Model Design

2.1   RAFForces

The objective of the implemented model was to have two forces; the RAF and the Luftwaffe, engage in an aerial battle over the English Channel, with the RAF fighters defending and trying to disrupt the incoming Luftwaffe attack. The various variables and agents associated with the RAF are summarized in Table 1. To allow altitude to be a consideration, the model was implemented in the 3D version of Netlogo [11].

2.2   German Forces

Table 2 summarizes the variables and agents associated with the Luftwaffe.

2.3   Model Functionality

The model's objective, and therefore its functionality, is centered around being able to answer the question of how the RAF could best arrange their forces to maximize the damage to the Luftwaffe, while minimizing their own damage. Therefore, at a high level the model must account for a defending force finding and then engaging the enemy, plus an offensive force that moves towards their assigned targets, that also has the ability to defend itself. In addition, the output of the model needs to provide key insights into the dynamics involved in producing the results in a more meaningful manner than the Lanchester model.

---

[3] In reality, this was not the case, as some RAF sorties were patrols that did not make contact with the enemy or were scrambled to meet a raid but failed to make contact. However, given the intent was to analyze actual combat performance the decision was made to ensure contact was made between the two forces.

Table 1. RAF variables and agents.

Variable	Purpose
Variables	
number_of_wings (wings)	The user selects the number of wings, between 1 and 5, that the FC scrambles. Each wing is assigned to a rally point and then has the fighters of a squadron(s) deployed to it. As per RAF standards, a squadron consists of 12 aircraft
squadrons_per_wing (sPW)	The user decides how many squadrons are assigned to each wing, as determined above. The option is again between 1 and 5. Therefore, the user can test Leigh-Mallory's single 'Big Wing' (5 squadrons per wing, which means scrambling 60 fighters) compared to Park's smaller multiple wings (1–2 squadrons per wing or 12–24 fighters per wing)
number_of_home_bases	The user sets the number of home bases that the FC forces are spread across. This allows the model to test for the implications of forming a large wing with fighters from multiple bases. This was a key consideration of the 'Big Wing' approach [10]. In the actual battle, 11 Group's had 27 squadrons who had access to 25 airfields, while 12 Group had 15 squadrons spread across 12 bases [2]
Agents	
Rally points	When initializing the RAF force, rally points are created first being spread evenly across the y axis (longitude) while having the same x (latitude) and z coordinates (altitude). These settings are independent from the coordinates of the incoming raid. As part of their initialization, RAF fighters are "hatched" by their rally point and allocated to a home base. Fighters form up at their rally point coordinates via the scramble routine. Rally points act as radar stations and direct their aircraft towards the enemy via the search routine, which covers 40 patches in a 360-degree arc
Home bases	Home bases are spread evenly across the y axis within the British mainland. RAF Fighters are assigned to a home base(s) nearest to their rally point. All fighters start a simulation at their home base
Hurricanes	The RAF has two classes of fighters. Hurricanes attack incoming bombers while Spitfires attack enemy fighters. This is consistent with the tactics of 11 Group [5]. Two key variables the fighters own are status and evading? The combination of these two determines the actions of a fighter. evading? has the value of **true** or **false**, while status can take the following values: **scramble, formation, engaged, searching, homebound** or **shot down**
Spitfires	Spitfires pursue enemy fighters. Note in this version of the model the different performance characteristics of the two fighters was not included

The RAF fighters' role was to intercept the incoming Luftwaffe wave(s) and destroy as many aircraft as possible, while avoiding being shot down, before returning to base. Figure 1 provides a flow chart of how the behavior of the RAF fighters was designed to meet this requirement along with other considerations of air combat.

The Luftwaffe fighters' primary role was to escort and defend their bombers. As mentioned above, the fighters would remain in formation until the number of RAF fighters around them exceeded their tolerance, at which point they would break off and attack the RAF. The Luftwaffe bombers' key objective was to find

Table 2. Luftwaffe Variables and Agents.

Variable	Purpose
Variables	
`ratio_to_RAF (r2RAF)`	The size of the Luftwaffe force is set as a ratio to the RAF force that has been scrambled to meet the incoming raid. In reality, the reverse would be true, but it ultimately makes no difference to the model. The ratio varied greatly throughout the battle as both sides altered tactics [1]
`ration_fighters_bombers` `(rationGFGB)`	The composition of a raid can be varied by the ratio of enemy fighters to enemy bombers. During the battle this ratio ranged from 3 fighters per bomber up to 5 [1]
`number_of_waves (waves)`	Sets the number of waves that the Luftwaffe is sending during a particular raid. [2] provides support for this value ranging between 1 and 3
`number_of_targets (targets)`	This sets the number of targets that the Luftwaffe pursue. The combination of `targets` and `waves` influences how compact or otherwise the raid is
Agents	
Targets	Targets are initialized with randomly created x and y coordinates within Britain. The coordinates are then assigned to the Luftwaffe force who track towards their allocated target
Waves	The initial class created for the Luftwaffe is a wave. Based on `waves`, their coordinates are set evenly along the y axis. Next aircraft are created for each of the waves. The number per wave is based firstly on the ratio of the Luftwaffe forces to the RAF (`r2RAF`), and then the number of waves. The aircraft's x and y coordinates are spread out in a formation around their wave's coordinates, while the fighters have a higher altitude (z coordinate) than the bombers
Bombers	The bomber class has the role of tracking to their target and once they reach it, dropping their bombs before returning home. The number of bomb hits is recorded in an attempt to judge the success of a raid. Bombers are also capable of defending themselves against the fighters. Bombers do not own the `evading?` variable and have formation, homebound or **shotdown** as their possible `status` settings
Fighters	The fighter's role is to defend the bombers. Each fighter has a tolerance variable and when the number of RAF fighters within a 4 patch radius exceeds their tolerance, they will break off and attack the RAF. The Luftwaffe fighters have the `evading?` variable. Their `status` includes **formation**, **engaged**, **shotdown** and **homebound**

their target, drop their bombs and then return home. An abbreviated illustration of how the Luftwaffe fighters' operated is provided in and Fig. 2[4].

The behavior of the agents is controlled by a combination of their **status** and **evading?** Variables. With the two forces having different objectives and procedures they require different set of statuses. The RAF fighters maintain

---

[4] Given the simplicity of the bombers role, it was felt a flow chart was unnecessary.

more possibilities because they are required to scramble, form their wing, find the enemy and engage. In contrast, the Luftwaffe fighters are already airborne and only need to find the enemy, before engaging. The requirements for the bombers are simpler again; as they head towards their target and defend themselves when attacked but do not change course. The agent sets do have some similar statuses, such as; shotdown and homebound. They also have some similar procedures, such as; checking whether they are being attacked and whether they have enough fuel to return home.

A high level flow of the model and therefore a description of Figs. 1 and 2 is;

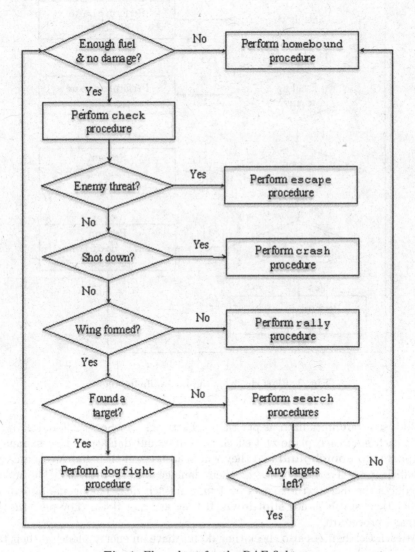

Fig. 1. Flow chart for the RAF fighters.

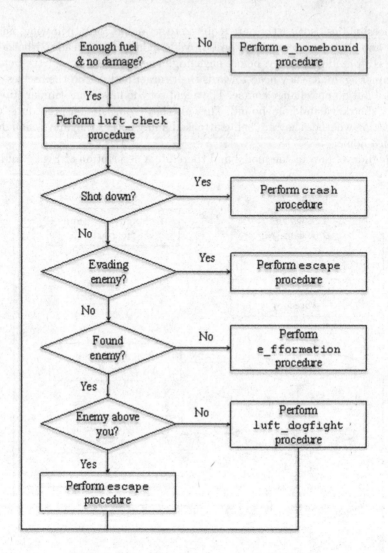

Fig. 2. Flow chart for the Luftwaffe fighters.

– Both sides are initialized as per the user settings (see Sects. 2.2 and 2.3),
– At each step each plane will check their fuel and damage. Their **status** is updated to **homebound** and they will head home if their fuel levels are just sufficient to get them home or their damage level is over 0.5. The model reduces the fuel for the agents by 1 unit at each tick. The agents also check that their status is not **shotdown**. If they are shot down they perform the **crash** procedure,
– At each tick fighters also check they do not have an enemy plane on their tail via their **check** procedure. If they do, the **evading?** variable is set to **true** and their opponent is set to 'nobody'. If a plane is required to evade it will

implement one of 5 strategies to move away from their threat. A plane cannot attack while they are evading the enemy. This procedure is consistent with the standard air battle tactic of breaking off an attack if you are in immediate danger of being shot down,

- Through the `rally` procedure the RAF scrambles their forces with the fighters climbing towards their assigned wing's rally point. All fighters have the `status` of **scramble** at this point and cannot engage the enemy,
- Once all the RAF fighters have reached their assigned rally point, the fighters have their `status` updated to **formation** and the wing is directed towards the incoming enemy wave(s) by their rally point and they are now able to attack. Rally points become aware of the exact coordinates of the incoming wave via their `search` routine which covers an area of 40 patches in a 360-degree arc,
- Once the rally point confirms the raid, through its `search` procedure, it will assign an enemy opponent to each of their fighters. The `status` of the fighters is updated to **engaged**.
- Meanwhile the Luftwaffe fighters have the `status` **formation**. At this point their `e_fformation` procedure has them moving towards the allocated targets of their bombers, while also being on the "look out" for the RAF. If they spot the RAF and the number of RAF fighters within a 3-patch radius is greater than their tolerance, their `status` is updated to **engaged**. However, if the RAF is above them they will take evasive action, through the `escape` procedure, before pressing an attack on the enemy. This is true of all offensive actions for both fighter forces and is an example of how the model utilizes basic air combat procedure,
- Once a fighter's `status` is updated to **engaged** their `dogfight` procedure is called with the sequence of an attack being; the attacking plane will set their heading and pitch to intercept their assigned opponent. This will either be a head on attack or the fighter will chase down their opponent from behind. When the attacker is close enough, within a 1 patch radius and within a 10-degree cone of sight, they will fire upon their opponent. The damage inflicted upon the opponent in the attack is a random float up to the value of 0.9. If a plane sustains damage above their survival level (.9) their `status` is updated to **shotdown**. The amount of damage inflicted per attack was determined by calibrating the model such that a representative battle of 24 RAF aircraft against 36 Luftwaffe aircraft recorded a similar loss ratio as an actual battle, which was around 5–10%,
- After the attack, the attacking fighter's `status` is changed. The RAF fighters are changed to **searching** while the Luftwaffe fighters change to **formation**, a status that ensures that the Luftwaffe is searching for the RAF. There are some minor differences in the search routines for the two fighter forces. While the RAF fighters check themselves for enemy fighters within 4 patches, if they cannot find any, they ask their rally point whether they are tracking any enemy planes, remembering the rally point has a broader search arc. If the rally point is tracking enemy targets, then it provides the coordinates of an enemy aircraft to their fighter, otherwise the battle is considered over and the RAF returns home via the **homebound** procedure. This process is consistent

with the RAF having the advantage of radar to assist in finding the enemy. In contrast, the Luftwaffe fighters are solely responsible for finding their own target and will return home after reaching the target, unless have sustained damaged or are running low on fuel,

- Enemy bombers continue towards their target with a number of fighters remaining in support. Bombers are able to protect themselves at each tick through their defend procedure. In this procedure a bomber selects any two fighters within a one-patch radius and fires upon them. To reflect the lower probability of hitting a fighter the damage inflicted is a random float up to .05, and

- When bombers reach their target they "unload" their bombs and return home. It should be noted that this step is simply a checkpoint with no consideration given to the amount of bombs that hit the target in this iteration of the model.

As detailed above, to achieve the objectives of the research question there was a certain amount of abstraction undertaken. However, while the actual movements of the aircraft might not match the exact characteristic of an air battle, the actions are supportable given the objectives of the agents and basic air battle tactics. There will always be the need for some abstraction in an ABM; otherwise you have you have moved beyond an ABM into an engineering model.

Verification of the model's behavior was undertaken by performing parameter sweeps on extreme values, with the results analyzed to ensure that the model was performing as per design. Extensive visual inspections were also undertaken, with the various agent classes color-coded based on status to ensure updating occurred as per the design.

3   Experiments

To understand the possible influences on the losses for both sides, a full factorial experiment (Experiment 1) combined with an analysis of variance (ANOVA) as outlined in [8] was undertaken. The design matrix, seen in Table 3, was used and generated 128 combinations, with each combination run 50 times in the simulation. From these settings the largest battle was 300 RAF fighters up against 1,200 Luftwaffe planes. While a battle like this did not occur, it highlights the benefits of creating a simulation capable of exploring the outcomes of such a battle. The mean of both the input and output variables from each combination was taken to form the values used in the ANOVA model. A principle component analysis (PCA) was undertaken on the data as well.

The settings in Table 3 are supported by the descriptions of various battles provided in [1,2,5]. In particular, the following points are relevant:

- The 'Big Wing' debate is all about determining whether 1 or 5 squadrons was the correct number of squadrons per wing. In addition, 11 Group had the flexibility of sending multiple wings, while 12 Group was restricted to 1. To maintain symmetry the range was set at 1 and 5, but it must be acknowledged that the RAF never deployed 5 wings of 5 squadrons,

Table 3. Design matrix for the full factorial experiment.

Variable	Low setting	High setting
numbaer_of_waves	1	3
number_of_wings	1	5
squadrons_per_wing	1	5
ration_fighters_bombers	3	5
ratio_to_RAF	1	4
number_of_home_bases	2	4
number_of_targets	1	3

– The size of the Luftwaffe force to the RAF varied throughout the course of the battle. Small raids, a ratio_to_RAF of 1, were used at the commencement of the battle before larger raids (a ratio of 4) were employed later in the battle,
– As mentioned previously the German's varied the ratio of fighters to bombers within the range of the experiment,
– The range of waves and targets is consistent with records of the battle, and
– Each RAF group had their planes spread across multiple bases, meaning that an intercepting wing was unlikely to be all from the same base; hence this variable ranges from 2 to 4. The author will concede that a combination of 1 squadron scrambling from 4 bases would not have occurred. However, the implications are minor, if any in this version of the model.

To assess the effectiveness of the 'Big Wing' approach, the results from 1 wing of 5 squadrons (1W5Ss) was compared against results from 5 wings of 1 squadron (5Ws1S) in Experiment 2. Each strategy was tested against an increasing German force ratio (r2RAF), with the ratio beginning at 1, moving to 4 in increments of 0.1. Fifty runs of the model were made at each ratio setting[5]. This scenario may not be 100% consistent with how 11 Group used their forces. However, to create a valid comparison, the author felt it was appropriate and necessary to ensure the British force size was consistent at 60 fighters.

An ordinary least squares (OLS) model as per Eq. 3 was fitted to the output of Experiment 1 and 2. Equation 3 provides the model for the British loss rate[6]:

$$\log\left(-\frac{dB}{dt}\right) = \log g + g1 \log GermanForces + b1 \log BritishForces \quad (3)$$

This approach is consistent with fitting the data to the aimed fire Lanchester model and replicates the analysis provided in [5]. An analysis of covariance (ANCOVA) was undertaken to establish whether a statistical difference existed between the resulting models from Experiment 2. All analysis was undertaken in R [9].

---

[5] The other settings used were 3 homebases, ratio_fighters_bombers 3, number_of_waves 2, number of targets 1 and ratio_spitfires_hurr 1.

[6] For Experiment 2 the British force was held constant, therefore the b1 term was dropped.

4 Results

Figure 3 presents the Biplot resulting from the PCA analysis. From the chart it can be seen that the first component (PC1), which had an explanatory power of 33%, relates mostly to the size of the forces engaged in the battle (RAFSize and GermanSize). Both the number of wings deployed and the number of squadrons per wing make a contribution. The second component (PC2), which explained 16.3% of the data, relates primarily to the ratio of the two force (r2RAF) contrasted against the number of German losses. This indicates that as the ratio of German planes to the British increased, their losses tended to decrease. This finding is inconsistent with what the Lanchester model prescribes. Further tests explore this finding.

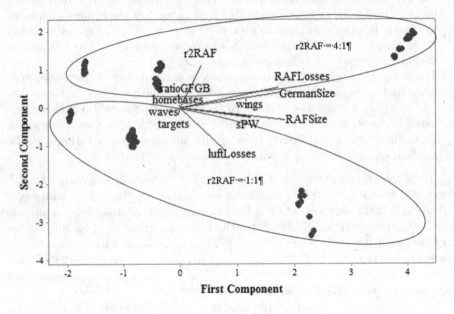

Fig. 3. Biplot resulting from the PCA analysis of the data from Experiment 1.

Also from Fig. 3 it can be seen that there is a clear division between where the data for raids with a 1:1 ratio sits (bottom half) compared to a 4:1 ratio (top half). The implications being that the British needed to match the force size of the Germans because while it increased the overall size of the battle, their losses were relatively lower when their ratio was closer to the Germans.

Table 4 presents the results of applying Eq. 3 to the full experimental data set. It should be noted that despite using the logs of the variables, both models failed the test for normality with regards to their residuals; hence the results are

Table 4. The results of fitting an OLS model to the data from Experiment 1.

Side	Variable	Estimate	Std.Error	t value	Pr(>|t|)
British	(Intercept)	−2.2732	0.0584	−38.90	0.0000
Losses	g1	0.8784	0.0502	17.49	0.0000
(Log)	b1	0.7854	0.0588	13.36	0.0000
German	(Intercept)	−0.0529	0.1158	−0.46	0.6488
Losses	b2	1.5201	0.1165	13.04	0.0000
(Log)	g2	−0.8842	0.0995	−8.88	0.0000

not robust. The British model, which returned an R^2 of 96.3%, is consistent with the Lanchester model in that the British losses scale positively with increasing force sizes from both sides, albeit at a rate less than one (the assumption of the aimed fire model). The results for the German losses are not consistent with the Lanchester model, with the model returning a negative coefficient for the impact of an increase German force. The interpretation of this result is that the German's benefited from safety in numbers – an increasing return to scale for safety. This result was most likely driven by the improved defensive performance of massed bombers and is consistent with the interpretation of the PCA analysis. The R^2 for the German model was 60.2%.

The results of the ANOVA and the subsequent OLS coefficients as per the approach of [8] are contained in Table 5. The dependent variable for the model was the British loss ratio (actual losses/the number of sorties), not the log of the actual losses, as per the previous model. The rationale for the change is that

Table 5. Results of the effect model fitted to the full factorial data set.

	Estimate	F-Value	t value	Pr(>|t|)
(Intercept)	0.2361	–	86.33	0.0000
ratio_to_RAF (r2RAF)	0.1290	2224.59	47.17	0.0000
number_of_wings (wings)	0.0945	1194.25	34.56	0.0000
squadrons_per_wing (sPW)	0.0999	1335.22	36.54	0.0000
number_of_waves (waves)	−0.0520	361.59	−19.02	0.0000
number_of_targets (targets)	−0.0192	49.48	−7.03	0.0000
r2RAF:wings	0.0459	282.33	16.80	0.0000
r2RAF:sPW	0.0564	425.88	20.64	0.0000
r2RAF:waves	−0.0352	165.83	−12.88	0.0000
r2RAF:targets	−0.0108	15.67	−3.96	0.0001
wings:sPW	0.0205	56.07	7.49	0.0000
waves:targets	0.0083	9.11	3.02	0.0031

the ratio normalizes the outcome across the various settings, thus enabling the identification of the key drivers. The R^2 of the regression model was 98.1%, with residuals meeting normality requirements.

From Table 5 it can be seen that there is significant interaction between r2RAF and the other variables, supporting the hypothesis that the FC needed to consider more than just force size in determining their strategies. This result is consistent with the influence of r2RAF in (PC2), as seen in Fig. 3. Other observations from Table 5 are:

1. Negative values for both r2RAF:waves and r2RAF:targets suggest that if an incoming raid is spread out, it benefited the British through a lower loss ratio;
2. Increasing the number of wings and sPW increased the British loss ratio as the Germans increased their force. This result provides mixed evidence in answering the 'Big Wing' debate. Experiment 2 provides greater insight on this point, and
3. The composition of the raiding party, the ratio of German fighters to bombers, the number of RAF home bases, were not significant factors.

Table 6 provides the results of fitting an OLS model explaining British losses as per Eq. 3 for the different strategies. The data was generated from Experiment 2 with the data illustrated in Fig. 4.

Table 6. Results of the effect model fitted to the full factorial data set.

Model	Variable	Estimate	Std.Error	t value	R^2
5Ws1S	(Intercept)	−0.6933	0.0622	−11.14	0.9682
	g1	0.8584	0.0289	29.69	
1W5Ss	(Intercept)	−1.0761	0.0616	−17.47	0.9777
	g1	1.0195	0.0286	35.64	

From Table 7 the results from the analysis of covariance (ANCOVA) and indicates that the interaction of the German force's size, and the number of wings (GF:Wing), is significant. This supports the hypothesis that the number of wings employed did indeed impact the loss rate of the British.

Table 7. Results of the ANCOVA testing for the significance of the two strategies.

	Estimate	F-Value	t value	Pr(>|t|)
(Intercept)	−1.0761	0.0619	−17.38	0.0000
g1	1.0195	0.0288	35.45	0.0000
Number of Wings (NW)	0.3828	0.0876	4.37	0.0001
LGF:NW	−0.1612	0.0407	−3.96	0.0002

Figures 4 illustrates the results of Experiment 2 by showing the relationship between the British and German losses versus the size of the German force, remembering that the German force increased against a set number of British fighters (60). Consistent with the findings from Experiment 1, an increasing German force results in greater British losses but lower German losses.

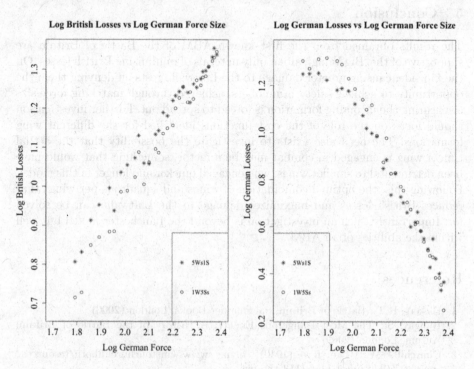

Fig. 4. (Left) Log plot of British Losses vs the log of the German forces. **(Right)** Log plot of German Losses vs the log of the German forces.

The results of Experiment 2 suggest that the rate of British losses scales at greater than one on average when the 'Big Wing' (1W5Ss) is employed, and less than one for the smaller wings (5W1S). This finding in isolation is indeed supportive of the strategy of Park. However, the smaller wing approach has a higher intercept value, with the interpretation being that the 'Big Wing' has a lower fixed cost yet higher variable cost of doing battle, while the smaller wing has the opposite. A similar analysis was undertaken on the German losses (Fig. 3) and there was no significant difference in the damage the British inflicted on the Germans by the two formations. The conclusion being that the British were limited in their ability to inflict greater losses on the Germans. Indeed, from the findings of Experiment 1, increased British successes were reliant on the German's waves spreading out.

Combining this inference with those from Experiment 1, it can be concluded that for the ranges that were tested for, the loss ratio of the British was higher under the smaller wing approach due to the average cost of the smaller wings being higher. Additionally, given there was no benefit from attacking in a smaller wing, it appears that when facing a German force equal to four times larger than the RAF force on average, the 'Big Wing' was the right approach.

5   Conclusion

The results obtained from the first known ABM of the Battle of Britain are supportive of the 'Big Wing', albeit only in terms of minimizing British losses. On the flip side, causing greater damage to the Luftwaffe rests on denying them the opportunity to achieve safety in numbers, achieved through matching force size or ensuring the incoming formation is forced to spread out. Further investigation should focus on the role of the cost functions identified for the different wing formations. The need also exists to investigate the possibility that the actual time a wing is engaged in combat may be a factor, something that would have been detrimental to smaller wings, who engaged quicker and longer in this model. Following this, the optimal combination of wings and squadrons per wings that reduces British losses and maximizes damage to the Luftwaffe can be solved for. Importantly, such an investigation is beyond the Lanchester model but well within the abilities of an ABM.

References

1. Bickers, R.T.: Battle of Britain. Salamander Books, London (2000)
2. Bungay, S.: The Most Dangerous Enemy: A History of the Battle of Britain. Aurum, London (2009)
3. Churchill, W.: The few (1940). http://www.winstonchurchill.org/resources/speeches/1940-finest-hour/113-the-few
4. Gowlett, P.: Assessing the military impact of capability enhancement with Netlogo using the Falklands War as a case-study (2013). http://www.mssanz.org.au/modsim2013
5. Johnson, I.R., MacKay, N.J.: Lanchester models and the battle of Britain. Naval Res. Logist. **58**(3), 210–222 (2011)
6. Lanchester, F.W.: Aircraft in Warfare: The Dawn of the Fourth Arm. Constable, London (1916)
7. MacKay, N., Price, C.: Safety in numbers: Ideas of concentration in Royal Air Force Fighter Defence from Lanchester to the battle of Britain. History **96**(323), 304–325 (2011)
8. NIST/SEMATECH. Nist/sematech e-handbook of statistical methods (2015). http://www.itl.nist.gov/div898/handbook/
9. R Development Core Team: A language and environment for statistical computing. R Foundation for Statistical Computing, Vienna (2015)
10. Sarkar, D.: Bader's Duxford Fighters: The Big Wing Controversy. Ramrod Publications, St Peter's, Worscester (1997)
11. Wilensky, U.: NetLogo (1999). http://ccl.northwestern.edu/netlogo/

Exploring Trade and Health Policies Influence on Dengue Spread with an Agent-Based Model

Damien Philippon[1(✉)], Marc Choisy[2,3], Alexis Drogoul[1], Benoit Gaudou[4],
Nicolas Marilleau[1], Patrick Taillandier[5], and Quang Chi Truong[1,6,7]

[1] UMI 209 UMMISCO, IRD, Bondy, France
damien.philippon.dev@gmail.com, alexis.drogoul@gmail.com,
nmarilleau@gmail.com
[2] UMR 34394 MIVEGEC, IRD, Montpellier, France
marc.choisy@ird.fr
[3] Oxford University Clinical Research Unit (OUCRU), Hanoi, Vietnam
[4] UMR 5505 IRIT, CNRS, University Toulouse 1 Capitole, Toulouse, France
benoit.gaudou@ut-capitole.fr
[5] UMR IDEES, University of Rouen, Rouen, France
patrick.taillandier@gmail.com
[6] CENRES and DREAM Team, Can Tho University, Can Tho, Vietnam
tcquang@ctu.edu.vn
[7] PDIMSC, University Pierre and Marie Curie/IRD, Paris, France

Abstract. With the globalization, several free trade areas have been and
are being created all around the world. They usually have positive consequences for increasing economic exchanges, but negative ecological or
health side effects. These negative effects are difficult to predict or even
to understand due to the complexity of the system and of the number of
involved processes. In this article, we focus on the Southeast Asia free trade
area (the ASEAN) and specifically in the East-West economic corridor. A
significant correlation has been observed in this area between the corridor
opening and dengue fever cases, without being able to establish a causality relationship. We choose to tackle this issue by building an agent-based
geographically explicit model. We propose an approach coupling dengue
fever dynamics, climate data, economic mobility and health policies, following a design methodology decomposing these processes in sub-models
and linking them to make one integrated model. In addition, we propose
a way to deal with lack of data in the modeling process. Our simulation
results show that there is influence of the increase in mobility and application of different control policies on the increase of dengue cases.

Keywords: Agent-based model · Epidemiological model · GIS data ·
Health policy

1 Introduction

Small countries have been forced to create associations or unions to compete in
the international marketplace, because of globalization. The first goal of these

© Springer International Publishing AG 2017
L.G. Nardin and L. Antunes (Eds.): MABS 2016, LNAI 10399, pp. 111–127, 2017.
DOI: 10.1007/978-3-319-67477-3_6

associations is to represent the countries as a unique economical area. To symbolize their union, the associations open free trade areas which help promoting internal trade by improving, for instance, their infrastructures or reducing taxes. Although these associations reach their goals of increasing good exchanges between countries, they also bring collateral effects that do not necessarily concern economy directly.

We chose to focus on the East-West Economic Corridor (EWEC) crossing Myanmar, Thailand, Laos and Vietnam, as it is a relatively small area with a lot of countries, different cultures but has also a strong economical trade area. A correlation link has been observed between the improvement of such infrastructures, by increasing the trade between countries and the number of dengue fever cases (cf. Fig. 1). Dengue is wide spread in Southeast Asia and a huge economic burden for the countries which fight it with heterogeneous policies. We chose to use an Agent-Based Model (ABM) to represent the problem, as it could offer the possibility to assess policies to combat dengue in silico, thus not interfering on the real environment without having a clear idea of the impacts that such policy may cause.

The contribution of this article is twofold. First, it presents a design methodology to build a complex model involving processes at different time and space scales in a context of limited available data. To deal with this shortage of data, we had to cross geographical data and epidemiological reports (to get dengue fever incidence by province, month and year) and scientific and institutional reports to estimate policies applied by countries. The proposed model combines an equation-based model for the disease dynamics, an individual microscopic mobility model and a policy application model at the country scale. Second, it presents a summary of the implemented model and discusses its results and its validation.

This paper is organized as follows. Section 2 presents the context of the case study with the presentation of the Association of Southeast Asian Nations (ASEAN) and of the EWEC corridor, a presentation of the dengue fever and and the different control policies employed to combat the mosquitoes in these different countries. Section 3 presents the methodology used, in particular concerning the collection of data and the implementation of the model. Section 4 is focused on the model itself, described using the O.D.D. Protocol [5]. Section 5 shows the results obtained and discusses them. At last Sect. 6 concludes and proposes some perspectives.

2   Context

2.1   ASEAN

ASEAN is composed of 10 countries of Southeast Asia including Indonesia, Thailand, Brunei, Cambodia, Lao PDR, Malaysia, Philippines, Myanmar, Singapore and Vietnam. This association aims at accelerate the economic growth and social progress of the concerned countries. The first plan was to establish a common internal market by promoting free trade, respecting agreements and collaborations. From this plan, different urbanisation projects between countries have been developed; one of them is the construction or improvement of economic corridors. In this study we are interested in the East West Economic Corridor, a corridor with its concept agreed in 1992 [12], built to promote the development of Myanmar, Thailand, Lao PDR and Vietnam and based on 1450 km of roads from Mawlamayine (Myanmar) to Da Nang (Vietnam). The corridor initially facilitates mainly the economy of the concerned countries, with new roads facilitating the transport of resources from one city to another along or near the corridor. But with the development of the corridor and the growth of trade among these countries (opening of the EWEC corridor the 12th December 2006), a collateral unwanted effect appeared: as the trade inside the corridor increased, so did the number of dengue fever cases. A correlation link have been made between these two data series but causality has not been proved yet (Fig. 1).

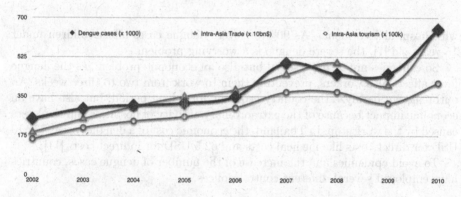

Fig. 1. Dengue cases and trade in the corridor.

2.2 Dengue Fever

The dengue fever is a disease which has an important incidence in the Asia Pacific: 75% of the world-wide population exposed to the dengue fever live in this area [9] (cf. Fig. 2). In the ASEAN, the number of cases has increased year after year over the last 10 years. This disease is a vector-borne disease, which means that its spread is only possible thanks to an organism, and in this case, two mosquito species: the *aedes albopictus* (a rural mosquito species) and the *aedes aegypti* (an urban mosquito species). An Infected mosquito bites a susceptible human being, which will lead to his/her infection. But human beings are also an infection source for the mosquitoes: an infected human being bitten by a susceptible mosquito will lead to its infection too.

The symptoms of the dengue fever are high fever, headache, pain behind the eyes, muscle and joint pains, nausea, vomiting, rash, and last for 2 to 7 days. But the real problems come with the severe dengue which can develop dengue shock syndrome in 30% of cases and is lethal in 20% of the cases (but only 1%

Fig. 2. Boosted Regression Trees (BRT) model probability of occurrence map. Map predicted at a 5 km × 5 km resolution with exclusion criteria [2].

with hospital treatment). As 90% of severe dengue cases affect children under 15 years old [7], the severe dengue is a worrying problem.

So countries are facing a social but also an economic problem, as the dengue fever affects also workers, preventing them to work from two to three weeks. An outbreak can paralyze the country economy for a long period, but also have an economic impact because of the extraordinary activity of hospitals and the losses caused by the work stop. In Thailand, the economic cost of a dengue case is 731.10 USD for direct costs like medical costs and 62.5 USD for indirect costs [11].

To avoid epidemics and the increase of the number of dengue cases, countries have employed several different control polices.

2.3   Health Policies

Health Policies or Control Policies denote all strategic choices of private (and in particular Non-Governmental Organisations (NGOs)) and public organisms aiming at improving health conditions of populations from whom they are responsible. A lot of existing Health Policies (cf. Fig. 3 for some examples) are available for countries with more or less efficiency and lower and higher cost depending on the area and population. Each country should make a trade-off between their budget, the cost of these policies and their effect on the population and on the disease spread. In the context of the dengue fever, Health Policies can be vector-control policies, which will, for example, reduce the number of mosquitoes in an area. They can also try to improve the Prevention and Education and tend to decrease the probability of being infected for the human population by putting mosquito nets, using repellents or simply advising population to wear long sleeve shirts.

Policies are not limited to cure and prevention systems, but include also anti-vector systems (cf. Fig. 3). We can consider four main kinds of anti-vector health policies: killing adult mosquitoes, preventing the breeding sites or killing larvae, preventing mosquito bites and preventing the virus transmission. All of these

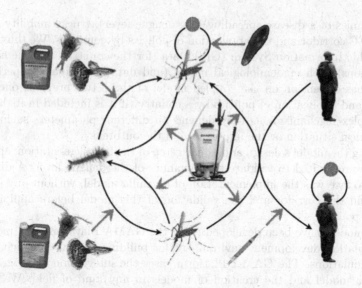

Fig. 3. Health policies available against dengue fever: guppy fishes to kill larvae, pesticide to kill adults or vaccine to prevent human infection...

Health Policies have the same goal: fighting against the dengue fever; however they use different means: killing adult mosquitoes relies more on pesticide, while reducing the number of mosquito bites relies on mosquito nets or on repellents.

Whereas all the means are more or less available to each country, real differences can be observed between countries in applied policies: for instance, in Asia, it is unthinkable to put chemicals inside the water tank, whereas in South America, it is unthinkable to put guppy fishes (a fish eating larvae) inside water tanks [6]. In the EWEC, there are two main causes for the differences in terms of policies applied. The first one is the kind of larvae breeding sites. In rural countries like Laos and Vietnam, the breeding sites correspond to water-holding containers, jars, which allow biological control by using fishes or mesocyclops when it is allowed and accepted by the communities. In urbanized areas, the breeding sites are flower pots, water dispenser troughs or even gutters, which do not allow application of policies like in rural areas. The second reason is the climate of each country. Southeast Asia proposes a large diversity of climates and each of them can increase or reduce the effects of a policy: in Vietnam, the mesocyclops coupled with bacteria killing larvae are showing better results than in Laos and Cambodia, where the guppy fish is more effective [6].

3   Methodology

3.1   Implementation of the Model

We chose to implement an ABM as it appears to be a good choice when we want to couple models from different domains. In our case, we are interested in the dynamics of a disease spreading (the dengue fever), trucks mobility among the EWEC corridor and the application of policies by countries. We thus couple Geographic Information System (GIS) Data (for the countries and meteorological stations) with epidemiological model (and data). We finally superimpose the policies dimension on the coupled model of those two previous ones. The decision and application of policies by a country (if it is included in its budget) are complex mechanisms as they depend on different parameters such as the geographical situation or the importance of the outbreak.

During the model's design and at each step of their implementation, epidemiologists were invited to validate the dynamics of the dengue fever. A difficulty we had to face was the implementation of a vanilla model, without any policies applied on the corridor and the validation of this model before applying the different policies.

The models have been developed using the GAMA Platform [4], a modeling and simulation development environment for building spatially explicit agent-based simulations. The GAMA Platform eases the integration of geographical data in a model and the creation of models in any kind of field. We choose this platform because it will make easier the launching of simulation with different geographical data: for instance, the model developed concerns the East West Economic Corridor, but the geographical files can be replaced by ones of another corridor, like the China-Pakistan economic corridor. The platform also makes possible the development and maintenance of submodels with different paradigms using different levels of abstraction like ODE, which is exactly in what we are interested in, and which is not easily done with its direct contender NetLogo [13].

3.2   Empirical Data

Building this model has required economical, epidemiological, meteorological, geographical data but also data about the different health policies used.

We get the economic data (i.e. exportation in dollars for each country with the other ones) and convert it into a number of trucks passing through the borders by giving a value in dollar to trucks. We make the assumption that those countries only exchange using terrestrial ways. This assumption comes from the idea that both maritime and aerial ways are used to exchange with other countries like China, but not for the countries in which we are interested. The destination of the truck always is a city, and the probability of this city to be chosen over the others depend on the population of the city. All these data were available on the website of the ministries of trade of the different countries. They are stored in a CSV file, with for each country its probability of export to another country of the corridor, its export budget and its economic growth for 2004 (Table 1).

The epidemiological data were provided by different ministries of health and contain the number of cases recorded by province, by month and by year. They are used to initialize the model. We use the incidence of the dengue fever of January, 2004 to initialize the model, mainly because it is a year in which we

Table 1. Probabilities of exportation for each country

	Vietnam	Laos	Thailand	Myanmar
Vietnam	0	0.12	0.86	0.02
Laos	0.33	0	0.66	0.01
Thailand	0.6	0.21	0	0.19
Myanmar	0.02	0.01	0.97	0

have data and it is before the opening of the corridor. An important point is that the data from Myanmar were not available.

The meteorological data were obtained from the website Climate-data.org[1]. This website provides information about different meteorological stations, recording temperature and rainfall by month. These data were used to compute the climate in the different cells of the cellular automata and are used in the emergence function of mosquitoes. We use the climate data of 2004.

The geographical shapefile data of the different countries, provinces, districts, cities and roads of the corridor come from OpenStreetMap website[2]. They represent 4 countries, 22 provinces and an area of 1500 km by 400 km (Fig. 4).

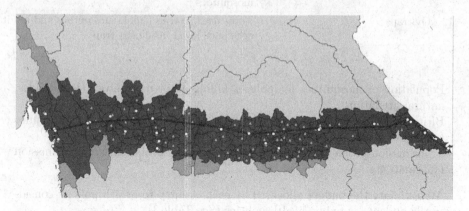

Fig. 4. Geographical representation of the Corridor with countries (yellow), provinces (green), districts (purple), cities (circles), weather stations (triangles) and the road. (Color figure online)

The data about the different policies (see Table 2) are more qualitative: they come from different articles and studies (mainly Community Based Dengue Vector Control [6]). Each policy will have effect on simplified parameters:

- Emergence of mosquitoes for policies which kill larvae (Environment management, Guppy fishes, BTI Briquets),

---

[1] http://climate-data.org.
[2] http://openstreetmap.org.

Table 2. List of the different policies possible

Id	Name of the Policy	Description
1	No policy	No policy will be applied
2	BTI briquets	Chemicals used to kill larvae inside water tanks
3	Natural predation	Guppy fishes are used inside water tanks to eat larvae
4	Natural preservation	Protection of the environment and the natural predators of the mosquitoes
5	Botanicals	Plants used to kill the mosquitoes
6	Mosquito nets	Nets used to prevent the mosquitoes from entering or biting people
7	Education	Formation, advertisements to inform people (removing water from pots for instance)
8	Environment management	Removing stagnant water sites near houses
9	Vaccines	Using the vaccination to immunize people from dengue
10	Insecticides	Aerosols used to kill adult mosquitoes
11	Genetically modified mosquitoes	Sterile male mosquitoes used to mate female mosquitoes
12	Ovitraps	Traps used to trap female mosquitoes and kill its eggs once layed inside the trap

- Population of mosquitoes for policies killing adult mosquitoes (insecticides, natural predation),
- Biting Rate for policies reducing the probability of being bitten by a mosquito (mosquito nets, long sleeves shirts),
- Transmission probability for policies reducing the probability of transmission (vaccination).

We estimate the budget allocated by each country to health policies considering the budget for public health policies (See Table 3).

Table 3. Health budget, rate between policy application and hospitalisation coverage, and policies applied by each country

	Budget	Proportion for policies	Hospitalisation cost per infected	Policies
Vietnam	13000000	0.44	64	2, 5, 6, 7
Laos	6000000	0.6	92.2	1, 4, 5, 6
Thailand	30000000	0.3	585	2, 5, 6, 7, 8
Myanmar	6000000	0.5	71	2, 3

4   Model

We present the model following the basic steps of the O.D.D. protocol [5]. Due to space limitation, we restrict ourselves to main parts of the protocol only.

4.1   Purpose

The aim of this model is to reproduce the dengue spread at the scale of the ASEAN East-West Economic corridor given the increase of trades between countries and provinces thanks to the corridor opening. We also aim at investigating the impact of the countries control policies.

4.2   Entities, Variables and Scales

As presented in Sect. 3.2, the considered reference system is an area of approximately 1500 km × 400 km, which groups a selected number of districts and provinces in Myanmar, Thailand, Laos and Vietnam along the East-West corridor with a population of millions of inhabitants and much more mosquitoes. The model starts in February 2004, with a time step duration of 12 h. There is no limit date that will stop the model, so that user can see the impact of policies in a long-term perspective.

Given this huge area, the fact that we do not have data to locate spatially each individual human being and animal and that case data are at the province scale, it is not relevant to model each individual. As a consequence, we will discretize the environment on a regular grid. Each `cell`, a 10 km square, will contain the number of human beings and mosquitoes in each infectious state and the parameters of the epidemic dynamics. The infection process will thus be performed at the cell scale. The population of human beings contained inside the cell is computed as follow: is if the cell contained a city, the population of the cell will be equals to the one of the city, else, it will be equals to the rural population of the district divided by the number of rural cells (cells not containing a city).

Trades in the corridor will be simply represented by economic exchanges between big cities through truck flows. Each individual `truck` agent will be able to carry infected people or mosquitoes and release them at their target city.

We add to this system `country` agents to manage health policies.

In addition, the model will contain several passive agents dedicated to integrating data in the model, such as `meteo station` dealing with temperature and rainfall data in the surrounding area, `district` and `province` agents to provide data about dengue case number and population and `city` and `road` agents to support truck mobility. The use of passive agents to embed data in the model is a very common modeling choice when dealing with socio-environmental systems (e.g. [3]). It allows the model to be homogeneous in terms of interactions between entities.

4.3 Process Overview and Scheduling

At each simulation step, the model does follow the same schedule. The countries apply their control policies on each cell. The epidemic dynamics is computed in each cell: it will update the (mosquito and human) population in each infection states. Finally the mobility process is executed to create new trucks, make them move to their targets and come back to their source. There is a small probability of epidemic interaction between truck and cells. All these processes are detailed in Sect. 4.5)

In addition, every year, countries update their global policy concerning dengue mitigation and the growth of country export is updated.

4.4 Initialization

At the initialization of the model, all the different processes use the data presented in Sect. 3.2 to define their initial state.

For the epidemiological part, we get from data the population of each country, province, district and city. However, we spread the population of human beings among the cells of the grid. We follow these steps:

1. each cell determines its district, if there is a city inside its shape and the closest meteorological station,
2. if the cell has a city, its population is immediately equal to the population of the contained city,
3. for all the other cells, we distribute homogeneously the remaining population of the district (i.e. the district population without the population of the cities),
4. each city receives the number of infected people of the province divided by the total number of cities of the province. If there is no city in the province, the number of infected people will be distributed among the cells with the highest population of the province,
5. finally, we compute the minimal number of mosquitoes needed to get the number of people infected in the cell using the number of people infected, the minimal number of bites that occurred to have this number of people infected with the probability of transmission given. As we know the minimal number of bites and the mean number of bites a mosquito can do, we can finally find the minimal number of mosquitoes needed.

For the mobility part, we just compute for each country the number of trucks needed for the year according to the export given for the current year and the estimated value of a truck. Using the probability of export, we can know how many trucks will go from one country to another country. To determine the origin and target cities for a truck, we consider the population of cities as a weight to determine the probability of the city to be chosen.

For the policy part, we follow these steps:

1. we use data to initialize the information about policies (their factor, their time of efficiency, their cost, the percentage of people to consider the policy applied as a success and their condition that the cell will have to check to apply the policy),

2. we use the lists of policies of each country and their budget to finally initialize the budget allocated for each policy by a country.

4.5 Submodels

Epidemiological Process. This process is based on two sub-processes: the first one spreads the disease to neighbour cells and the second one computes the evolution of humans and mosquitoes infectious states in the current cell. Given the time scale, we needed to represent explicitly mosquitoes population and its life-cycle because, depending on the season the number of mosquitoes can be extremely different and so is the number of new dengue cases. In addition, the various Health Policies do have an effect on mosquitoes depending on their state.

Each day a small rate of the cell mosquito population is thus exchanged with neighbour cells. Although mosquitoes have a very small move range, this represents mosquitoes population at the border of two cells[3].

We choose a compartment Ordinary Differential Equations (ODE) model for the disease dynamics (in particular because we choose to gather in a single entity, the cell, the human beings and mosquitoes populations, so each cell contains an ODE system, interpolated using Range Kutta 4 method). It is based on the model proposed by [8]. We have 2 populations: the mosquitoes and the human beings (cf. Fig. 5): human beings can be in 4 states (Susceptible, Exposed, Infected and Recovered). Once a human being is recovered from the dengue, it cannot be infected by the same serotype. But as there are 4 serotypes of dengue, we consider that a recovered human can become susceptible again (this represent the fact that a human being is susceptible to other serotypes). Mosquitoes can be only in 3 states (Susceptible, Exposed and Infected) as they cannot recover. As shown in the Fig. 5, humans become infected because of an infected mosquito and conversely.

The evolution of this model is described using the following ODE systems (left column for the mosquito dynamics, right column for the human beings one):

$$\frac{dS_v}{dt} = h_v(S_v + E_v, t) - \lambda_v(t)S_v - \mu_v S_v \qquad \frac{dS_h}{dt} = -\lambda_h(t)S_h + \omega_h R_h$$

$$\frac{dE_v}{dt} = \lambda_v(t)S_v - \upsilon_v E_v - \mu_v E_v \qquad \frac{dE_h}{dt} = \lambda_h(t)S_h - \upsilon_h E_h$$

$$\frac{dI_v}{dt} = h_v(I_v, t) + \upsilon_v E_v - \mu_v I_v \qquad \frac{dI_h}{dt} = \upsilon_h E_h - \gamma_h I_h$$

$$\frac{dR_h}{dt} = \gamma_h I_h - \omega_h R_h$$

---

[3] We choose to represent the diffusion process through mosquitoes exchanges in order to stay simple and more flexible if we want to change the simulation step length: in particular it avoids us to take into account commuting process when simulation step length is lower than 1 day and we want to represent spread diffusion through human migrations.

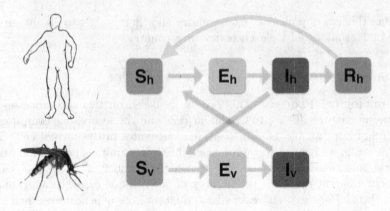

Fig. 5. SEIRS-SEI compartment model for dengue contamination

with: $\lambda_v(t)$ (resp. $\lambda_h(t)$) the transfer rate from Susceptible to Exposed for the vector (resp. human beings), v_v (resp. v_h) the transfer rate from Exposed to Infected for vectors (resp. human beings). γ_h (resp. ω_h) is the transfer rate from Infected to Recovered (resp. Recovered to Susceptible) for human beings. Given the time scale of the simulation we take into account demography only for the vector: h_v is the emergence rate given a population and the time t and μ_v is the vector mortality rate. This emergence function comes from [10]: the population increase rate is a function of the temperature and rain given a double Poisson distribution.

Trade Exchange Submodel. We made the hypothesis that we can represent trade exchange by taking into account only the commercial trucks mobility carrying goods between cities. The trade exchange model requires thus 3 steps at 3 different time scales:

1. (Each year) Update of each country economic growth and of the export value.
2. (Each day) Truck creation: each country, based on its export value, creates a number of trucks in their cities and provides them with targets in other countries.
3. (Each simulation step) Truck movement: trucks move back and forth from their origin to their target (and conversely) and are removed when they come back.

The truck movement takes benefits of the GAMA platform features that provide built-in functions to deal with agents move on a (road) graph (given an agent speed and simulation step length).

Policy Submodel. We make the hypothesis that control policies are decided and managed at the country level. Each country has a given amount of money they can use either to cure people or to invest in control policies. A policy is applied on each cell and has an impact on disease dynamics parameters. Among all the existing policies, each country only uses a subset (for practical, financial or cultural reasons). The dynamics of the model obeys a 3-step process:

1. (Each year) Reallocate budget: each country computes the budget allocated to control and to hospitalisation and to each policy (same algorithm as for the initialization).
2. (Each day) Apply policies: each country computes for each of its policy:
   - if it can be applied (depending on the period and of remaining budget) on each cell,
   - the impact of the policy application on disease dynamics and spread parameters.
3. (Each day) Update budget: each country computes the cost of its policy and updates its budget.

   Each country has a set of policies to apply.

5   Results and Discussion

The main result of this model is to be able to show that there is a correlation relationship between the evolution of the economic exchanges and the evolution of Dengue cases (in the West-East ASEAN corridor area). Figure 6 shows the results in four different cases: with or without mobility and with or without policies. The red and blue curves show unrealistic cases where policies would not be applied. The only goal of these scenarios is to show that without policies, the mobility has only an impact on the spreading speed of the disease, allowing the disease to reach its maximal incidence faster. The green and yellow curves are more realistic. The yellow one shows the incidence of the disease without mobility (only the one for mosquitoes is present), which corresponds more or

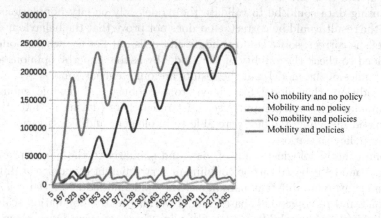

Fig. 6. Results of different experiments: the figure shows the number of Dengue cases given the step number (one step is one day). (Color figure online)

less to the region before the setting up of the corridor. The green one represents the incidence of the disease with the setting up of the corridor, facilitating those outbreaks. We can observe the huge impact of policies application on Dengue cases number. We can also observe a speeding up effect of the mobility on the case number evolution.

The goal of the model is not to show that reducing the mobility along the corridor would help to fight against dengue fever, but to explain the correlation between the growth of dengue cases and the growth of trade between the different countries. The mobility has certainly an effect on the dengue fever spread, however, it also provides funds for the concerned countries, which can be used for the health policies.

As we can see in Fig. 7, if a country uses different policies, it would have consequences for all the countries among the corridor. By applying the policies of Myanmar, Laos reduced the number of dengue cases within the corridor (precisely with Thailand and Vietnam as Laos does not trade a lot with Myanmar, and the trucks do not pass through Myanmar too).

We have checked the validity of the model and of its results at various steps. First, the conceptual model has been designed together with an expert in epidemiology and in particular in Dengue fever, which ensures that assumptions made are correct. The model has then been carefully implemented, each sub-process being tested separately and then coupled. Finally we made an attempt to validate the model using real data.

A problem concerning this validity of the model raised. The first way to validate the model would be to compare the number of infected people inside the model and the data we have for each month by province. However, the data available are only for the hospitals of the provinces, which can have false positive or true negative data. But these numbers do not take into account the rural population of the provinces: the rural population is most of the time poorer than the urban population, which prevent the human beings to go to hospital to be cured, and thus the cases are not recorded. Another method to validate the model using data could be to validate the model only on city populations: but even if the result would be correct, that does not prove that the behaviour of the rural cells is correct, so we could validate city cells but not the whole model. So we decided to check the validity of the model by asking experts' opinions about the dynamics of the model and the results are quite encouraging.

In addition, this model has shown to be robust and flexible enough to be manipulated by non-computer scientist researchers (during an initiation to agent-based modeling[4]). They were able to implement and assess various coordination policy scenarios.

From a methodological point of view and similarly to the model presented in [1], our model is based on the coupling of very different dynamics at different scales and involving different paradigms: the epidemic model at the cell scale, based on a macroscopic ODE-based model working at the population scale and the individual truck mobility model. Coupling these two paradigms allow us to

---

[4] The Tam Đao Summer School in Social Sciences (JTD) www.tamdaoconf.com/.

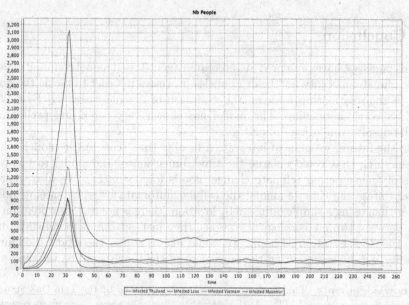

(a) Laos Applying its policies

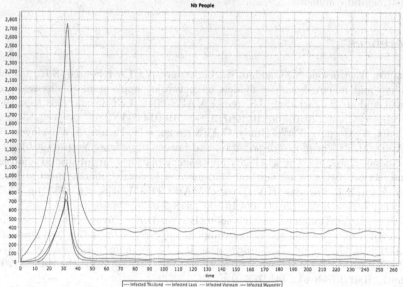

(b) Laos Applying Myanmar Policies

Fig. 7. Different policies for Laos

apply processes at the scale of a population (of millions of individuals) and at the scale of individuals.

6 Conclusion

In this paper we have presented an integrated agent-based model coupling dengue fever, climate, mobility and health policies processes in order to tackle the question of the relationship between the evolution of dengue cases and East-West ASEAN corridor opening. The model has shown very promising preliminary results despite validation difficulties.

In the future, we plan to integrate a flexible time scale in the model, which is something that could enlarge the time dimension of the model to use it in cases of longer period (climate change, floods for instances). We also want to better diffuse the climate among the cellular automata by using satellites data rather than using a simple diffusion by location (there is not any interpolation for cells between two meteorological stations, they just get the meteorological data from the closest station). Finally, we would like to add in the model the human mobility, e.g. by representing the movement of the tourists or the workers.

Acknowledgements. This work was part of and supported by the Tam Dao Summer School in Social Sciences (JTD). Authors want to thank the three anonymous reviewers for their helpful comments.

References

1. Banos, A., Corson, N., Gaudou, B., Laperrière, V., Coyrehourcq, S.R.: Coupling micro and macro dynamics models on networks: application to disease spread. In: Gaudou, B., Sichman, J.S. (eds.) MABS 2015. LNCS, vol. 9568, pp. 19–33. Springer, Cham (2016). doi:10.1007/978-3-319-31447-1_2
2. Bhatt, S., Gething, P.W., Brady, O.J., Messina, J.P., Farlow, A.W., Moyes, C.L., Myers, M.F.: The global distribution and burden of dengue. Nature (2013)
3. Gaudou, B., et al.: The MAELIA multi-agent platform for integrated analysis of interactions between agricultural land-use and low-water management strategies. In: Alam, S.J., Parunak, H.V.D. (eds.) MABS 2013. LNCS, vol. 8235, pp. 85–100. Springer, Heidelberg (2014). doi:10.1007/978-3-642-54783-6_6
4. Grignard, A., Taillandier, P., Gaudou, B., Vo, D.A., Huynh, N.Q., Drogoul, A.: GAMA 1.6: advancing the art of complex agent-based modeling and simulation. In: Boella, G., Elkind, E., Savarimuthu, B.T.R., Dignum, F., Purvis, M.K. (eds.) PRIMA 2013. LNCS (LNAI), vol. 8291, pp. 117–131. Springer, Heidelberg (2013). doi:10.1007/978-3-642-44927-7_9
5. Grimm, V., Berger, U., DeAngelis, D.L., Polhill, J.G., Giske, J., Railsback, S.F.: The ODD protocol: a review and first update. Ecol. Model. **221**(23), 2760–2768 (2010)
6. Lloyd, L.S., Beaver, C., Seng, C.M.: Managing regional public goods for health community-based dengue vector control. Technical report, Asian Development Bank, World Health Organization (2013)

7. Malavige, G., Fernando, S., Fernando, D., Seneviratne, S.: Dengue viral infections. Postgrad. Med. J. **80**(948), 588–601 (2004)
8. Manore, C.A., Hickmann, K.S., Hyman, J.M., Foppa, I.M., Davis, J.K., Wesson, D.M., Mores, C.N.: A network-patch methodology for adapting agent-based models for directly transmitted disease to mosquito-borne disease. J. Biol. Dyn. (2015)
9. Murray, N.E.A., Quam, M.B., Wilder-Smith, A.: Epidemiology of dengue: past, present and future prospects. Clin. Epidemiol. **5**, 299–309 (2013)
10. Parham, P., Michael, E.: Modeling the effects of weather and climate change on malaria transmission. Environ. Health Perspect. **118**(5), 620–626 (2010)
11. Shepard, D.S., Undurraga, E.A., Halasa, Y.A.: Economic and disease burden of dengue in southeast asia. PLoS Negl. Trop. Dis. **7**(2), e2055 (2013)
12. The Centre for Logistics Research in Thammasat University. The GMS east west economic corridor logistics benchmark study. Technical report, Thammasat University (2016)
13. Wilensky, U., Evanston, I.: Netlogo. Center for connected learning and computer based modeling. Technical report, Northwestern University (1999)

Extracting Movement Patterns from Video Data to Drive Multi-Agent Based Simulations

Muhammad Tufail[1]([⊠]), Frans Coenen[1], and Tintin Mu[2]

[1] Department of Computer Science, University of Liverpool, Liverpool L69 3BX, UK
imtufail@liv.ac.uk
[2] Department of Electrical and Electronics Engineering, University of Liverpool,
Liverpool L69 3BX, UK

Abstract. Computer simulations are used to create and evaluate real world scenarios in a manner that is controlled, non intrusive, cost effective and safe. One technology for realising computer simulation is Multi Agent Based Simulation (MABS), the advantage being that the entities that feature in a simulation can be expressed as agents that have all the features associated with agents (autonomy, goal driven, etc.). A particular challenge of MABS is the acquisition of the data required to define agent behaviour. One approach is to "hand craft" agent behaviour, however this is error prone and time consuming. In this paper we proposed a method whereby we can extract, what we have termed "Movement Patterns" (MPs) which in turn can be used to drive agents in a MABS environment.

Keywords: Multi Agent Based Simulation (MABS) · Movement pattern mining · Movement Patterns

1 Introduction

Multi-Agent Based Simulation (MABS) harnesses Multi Agent System technology to realise computer simulations of real world scenarios. MABS offers the fundamental advantage that the entities that make up a simulation can be modelled as agents which display all the characteristics of agents. Using MABS each "player" in the simulation is represented as an agent. These agents posses both desires and capabilities, which in turn allows autonomous operation and decision making. MABS is particularly appropriate for modelling scenarios that involve people or animals [2,5,6]; each person (animal) can be modelled as an agent.

The MABS application domain of interest with respect to this paper is behaviour analysis, more specifically animal movement behaviour analysis. Examples where MABS have been used for human behaviour analysis can be found in [3,7,8]. The challenge of behaviour MABS is the modelling of individual agent behaviours. One approach [2] is to "hand craft" the models on which the agent behaviour will be based by observing the real world entities to be considered. However, hand crafting is error prone and resource intensive. An alternative,

L.G. Nardin and L. Antunes (Eds.): MABS 2016, LNAI 10399, pp. 128–140, 2017.
DOI: 10.1007/978-3-319-67477-3_7

and that advocated in this paper, is to use data mining techniques to learn the desired agent behaviours in an automated manner. More specifically to apply such techniques to video data, featuring the entities (agents) of interest in the intended environment, and learning the desired behaviour in the form of patterns as first proposed in [15]. This paper extends the work presented in [15] by proposing a mechanism for mining video data to extract "Movement Patterns" (MPs), which in turn can be used in the context of animal movement behaviour MABS. MPs in this context are spatially referenced patterns that specify potential follow on locations for a given agent (animal), however MPs can be applied in the context of other movement behaviour studies such as fire exit simulation and movement behaviour at rail terminal/station forecourts or airport concourses. MPs can be defined in absolute terms according to some reference origin; or in relative terms according to the nature of an agent's current location. MPs are selected in a random probabilistic manner so that on each run the behaviour of agents will not be identical. The main contributions of the work presented in this paper are thus: (i) a mechanism for capturing MPs, and (ii) a mechanism whereby MPs can be effectively utilised in a MABS setting.

The rest of this paper is organised as follow. An overview of some previous work is presented in Sect. 2. In Sect. 3 the process of data acquisition and the nature of the video data used for illustrative purposes with respect to this paper is discussed. The environment representation, an important precursor to any discussion on MPs, is presented in Sect. 4, followed by the pattern mining framework itself in Sect. 5. Section 6 discusses a proposed MABS framework which utilises the concept of MPs. Section 7 then presents an evaluation of the operation of the proposed MABS in terms of MPs. A summary and some conclusions are presented at the end of this paper, together with some suggestions for future work, in Sect. 8.

2   Previous Work

Computer simulation offers a number of advantages over real life experimentation. The main challenge of MABS, as in the case of computer simulation in general, is the acquisition of the knowledge required to build the simulations. In [1], this was done by hand, an approach found to be very resource intensive; rodent behaviour was modelled using the concept of a behavioural graph. Hand crafting is thus both time consuming and error prone. An alternative approach was considered in [15] where the idea was to learn the behaviours of agents from video data and then to utilise this in a MABS setting. In [15] only single mouse scenarios were considered which served to significantly simplify the nature of the models to be considered. In this paper a more sophisticated mechanism in the context of multiple agents is presented.

The proposed use of MPs, as will be seen later in this paper, includes the concept of *states* to represent the relationship between entities in a MABS. The idea of states has for some time been used in the context of simulation, and by extension, MABS; although it should be noted that in previous work the concept has not been used in the same way as presented in this paper. In previous work a state typically describes a set of attribute-values that an agent possesses at a given time t_1; a follow on state is then a potential future state that an agent may adopt at time t_2. With respect to behaviour simulation, in [5, 10, 14] the concept of states has been used to represent the behaviour of entities. For example in [5] states were used for the representation of animal behaviour, more specifically foraging of sheep. In [10] states were used to represent the way that a group of ants selected a "best" nest site, although the group was considered in terms of a single entity. In our case the state concept is used to capture the relative position of two mice (as discussed further in Subsect. 4.2 below).

The fundamental idea presented in this paper is that the necessary knowledge can be derived from video data through a video data analysis process. More specifically the idea is to extract "movement patterns" from video data and utilise these patterns to drive a MABS.

3   Data Acquisition and Video Data Collection

When building a MABS the most challenging task (as noted earlier) is the acquisition of the knowledge required to populate the simulation. This section discusses the acquisition of data; more specifically extracting knowledge from video data. From the literature different methods have been proposed concerning data acquisition. The usually process is one of observation or interviews with domain experts. For example in [10] a set of behavioural rules were derived through a process of observation, and in [13] surveys of individuals were conducted. In [12] the following observations were made concerning the manual processes of MABS data acquisition:

1. It is difficult to translate information gleaned from domain experts (or from observations) into usable form since such translation typically requires extensive domain knowledge.
2. Any hypotheses concerning agent behaviour, based on information obtained from domain experts (or derived from laboratory experiments) needs to be precise (information gleaned from domain experts is typically "fuzzy").
3. The manual collection of data from real world scenarios, regardless of how this is done, is a time consuming and resource intensive process.

The most significant of the above is that manual data acquisition is a resource intensive process and thus some form of automation is desirable. In [13] the authors briefly discuss the potential for automatically extracting the required data from existing records (documents); in this paper it is suggested that the automated extraction of knowledge from video data is the solution.

Recall that the focus for the work presented in this paper is scenarios involving two or more mice in a "box environment" (as in [15]). To this end video data was obtained in a laboratory setting by suspending a video camera over a box, whose ground area measured $1.2\,m^2$, into which two mice and some objects (nests, obstructions and so on) were introduced. Two stills from the video data collected are given in Figs. 1 and 2; in the figures the two mice can be clearly identified. Note that the stills feature slightly different scenarios; the obstructions are not in the same place in both cases. The circular objects are nests which mice can enter and exit. The boxes also feature side panels but these are not of significance with respect to the desired video analysis.

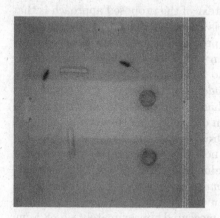
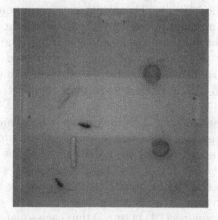

Fig. 1. Still from rodent video data (example 2)

Fig. 2. Still from rodent video data (example 2)

For the work presented in this paper a bespoke software system was developed, for tracking "mice" in video data, founded on the "blob tracking" technique[1]. The software operates by processing the video data in a "frame by frame" manner. The software automatically detects the location of each mouse by detecting movement and then assigning a tracking ID to the identified blob. Blob locations are recorded at a fixed *sample interval time s* measured in term of a number of video frames. With respect to the work presented in this paper $s = 5$ frames was used (5 frames equates to 200 ms). On occasion the blob tracking fails due to noise in the data or because the blob "disappears" into a nest. Where this happens the initialisation process is repeated and, once the blob has been re-identified, the tracking ID is reassigned.

The situation where both mice were lost at the same time did not occur, but erroneous reassignment of IDs would not adversely effect the data collection and the consequent mining of MPs. At the end of the mouse tracking process two sets of locations were obtained, one for each ID (more if scenarios featuring a greater number of mice are considered). The learning process continues until we have at least one MP for every potential location. In this paper we discuss two

---

[1] available at:
  https://nsl.cs.usc.edu/enl/trunk/aqua/OpenCV-2.3.1/doc/vidsurv/Blob_Tracking_Modules.doc, https://nsl.cs.usc.edu/enl/trunk/aqua/OpenCV-2.3.1/doc/vidsurv/Blob_Tracking_Tests.doc.

mechanism for representing locations, absolute and relative, both are considered in further detail in Sect. 5.

4 Environment Modelling

An important aspect of MABS is the nature of the environment (playing area) to be modelled [9]. The significance in the context of the proposed approach is that the mechanism whereby the environment is modelled influences the nature of the output from the machine learning. The proposed representation is essentially that of a "tile world" (such as that used in [4,11]). Using this mechanism the environment is modelled by dividing it into a collection of grid cells (squares). Each cell is given a sequential number (*address*); the set of grid numbers is then given by $L = \{l_1, l_2, l_3 \dots\}$. Grid mechanisms of this form offer the general advantage that prescribed translations from one cell to another can be achieved by applying a constant k to the current address (a concept also used in [15]). For example, in Fig. 3, to move one cell to the north $k = -14$; and to move one cell to the south east $k = 15$. Note that the value of k captures both distance and direction, hence we refer to such values as *movement vectors*; $k = 0$ indicates no movement. For the video data the $1.2\,\mathrm{m}^2$ environment was divided into 14×14 grid squares (196 in total); thus each square measured approximately $8.5 \times 8.5\,\mathrm{cm}$, about the size of a mouse.

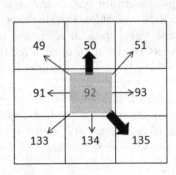

Fig. 3. Movement vectors

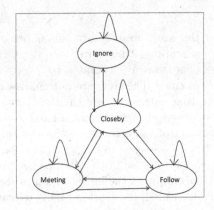

Fig. 4. State graph

As will become clear later in this paper two kinds of MP are considered, relative and absolute. For relative MPs each grid cell describing an environment has a ground type associated with it. Five ground type labels were used $\{w, n, b, o, -\}$; where: w indicates a location next to a wall, n indicates a nest site, b indicates an obstruction of some kind (a "block"), o indicates "open ground" (and is also the default label) and $-$ indicates an area outside of a playing area. Similar ground type labels were considered in [15].

4.1   Location Descriptors

A location descriptor is a *composite ground type* label comprised of the ground types for the 3×3 sub grid surrounding current location of interest linearised from top-left to bottom right. Recall from Sect. 4 that we have a ground type − indicating locations outside of a playing area, this is used in the case of corner and edge locations.

4.2   States

An important aspect of the proposed framework is the concept of states. As noted above, in the context of this paper, a state defines the relationship between two entities (mice in our case) in such a way that this can be incorporated into MPs. We have four different states {"ignore", "closeby", "meeting", "follow"} arranged in a graph as shown in the Fig. 4. The states are defined on the basis of: the distance between the two entities in term of "zones" surrounding each entity, the direction of one to the other and their mutual directions of travel.

5   Movement Pattern Mining Framework

The objective of the proposed MP mining framework is to extract (mine) MPs from the location data obtained as a result of the video analysis described in Sect. 3. For each entity (mouse) and each sample time stamp t_i we extract a MP describing the entity's movement from t_i to t_{i+1}.

As discussed previously, two mechanisms were considered for representing MPs: (i) absolute and (ii) relative. The distinction between the two, as the terminology suggests, is that in the first case locations are recorded relative to the origin of the environment while in the second locations are recorded relative to the local surroundings. Absolute locations are therefore expressed in terms of a specific address (a unique number), while when using relative patterns the locations are represented using descriptors. The significance is that absolute patterns can only be used with respect to simulations that feature the same environment as that from which the patterns were mined, while relative patterns are more versatile and can be used for a variety of simulations. However, relative descriptors are more complex. The advantages of using relative patterns over absolute patterns are as follows: (i) fewer location pattern are required than the number of cells in the grid (given a reasonably sized paying area), (ii) consequently storage advantages are accrued, (iii) they are more generic than the absolute mechanism (MBPs represented using the absolute mechanism can only be used with respect to a playing area identical to that from which they were extracted) and (iv) they are rotation invariant.

In this section both mechanisms are considered in further detail in the context of MPs. It should also be noted here that the extracted MPs provided a "knowledge base" with which to drive the desired MABS. The operation of this

MABS is presented in the following section, Sect. 6. The fundamental structure of an MP is that of a tuple of the form:

$$MP = \langle F, S, v, Path \rangle$$

where: (i) F is the "From" location (where the movement represented by the MP starts); (ii) S is a collection of one or more states describing the spatial relationship between agents featured in a scenario; (iii) v is a *movement vector* (as described in Sect. 4); and (iv) $Path$ is the *path*, encapsulated by the MP, which an agent needs to follow to get to the "To" location. The nature of these elements is discussed in further detail in the remainder of this section.

The From location (F) is the start location in the grid environment from where the movement described by a MP commences, defined in terms of a location identifier loc_ID. The format of loc_ID depends on whether we are considering absolute MPs or relative MPs. In the first case it will simply be a grid cell number, in the second case it will be a location descriptor of the form described above in Subsect. 4.1.

Each state s in S defines the relative relationship between two agents using a set of labels, {"ignore", "closeby", "meeting", "follow"} defined using a set of concentric zones as explained in Subsect. 4.2. An MP can feature one or more states depending on how many agents feature in a scenario. If we have n agents then $S = \{s_1, s_2, \ldots, s_{n-1}\}$, we are not interested on how an agent relates to itself hence $n-1$. If there is only one agent, then $S = \emptyset$. Note that a MP defines movement in terms of a single entity.

The element v of the MP tuple is a movement vector of the form described in Sect. 4. The value for v can be expressed as a single number or as a coordinate pair $\langle x, y \rangle$ depending on whether we are using absolute or relative MPs. The value of v when applied to an agent's current location indicates the "To" location associated with the MP.

The fourth component, $Path$, as already noted, indicates the "route" that the MP prescribes whereby an agent adopting the MP can get from its From location to the indicated To location. The number of elements in $Path$ ($|path|$) depends on how far we wish to "look ahead". With respect to the evaluation and case studies presented later in this paper $|path| = 5$ was used. Using $|path| > 1$ means that our rodent agents have a "memory", they have a planned route they wish to follow. The elements of $Path$ are all movement vectors. Thus using absolute movement patterns, where $|path| > 1$, we have a sequence of movement vectors of the form $\{v_1, v_2, \ldots, v_{|path|}\}$ were $v_{|path|}$ indicates the end location (the To location) and the remaining vectors indicate locations at intermediate locations referred to as *waypoints*. In the case of relative movement patterns, where $|path| > 1$, we have a sequence of movement vectors of the form $\{\langle x_1, y_1 \rangle, \langle x_2, y_2 \rangle, \ldots, \langle x_{|path|}, y_{|path|} \rangle\}$.

6   Operation of MPs in the Context of MABS

This section describes how MPs are integrated into our proposed MABS framework. Our MABS, like other MABS, operates in an iterative manner. On each iteration each agent featured in the current scenario of interest updates its location, direction and current path. This is done according to whether we have waypoints pending or not. In the first case $|Path| > 1$ and the next location $w_i \in Path$ can be selected (and removed from $Path$). This process continues until $|Path| = 0$ is reached. When $|Path| \equiv 0$ a new MP must be selected.

In the evaluation considered later in this paper each MABS agent uses the same knowledge base, but this does not have to be the case. Agents search the knowledge base with their current location (described in absolute or relative terms) and State and identify all relevant MPs and consequent To locations. Typically there will be a number of these. Given that we do not wish our simulation to operate in the same manner on each run a specific MP is selected in a probabilistically weighted random manner. In other words the most likely MP is the most likely to be selected but not necessarily so. In the case of relative patterns it is also necessary to carry out additional checks to make sure that associated To locations are *legal* locations. A legal location is one within the environment (thus not a location with ground type $-$) that is not obstructed in some way (thus not a location with ground type b). Note that on start up our mouse agents are placed at some legal location and their states set according to their relative positions in the simulation environment. Note also that in the case where no legal follow on location can be found a default next location will be selected (in practice we found that this situation did not occur).

Simulation time was calculated according to Eq. 1. Simulations should operate so that the agents move in a smooth manner from one location to another location. In Eq. 1, q is some constant; with respect to the evaluation presented later in this paper $q = 5$ was used as this was found to produce a smooth simulation. Recall that the sample time was 200 ms, thus with respect to this paper simulation time was $200/5 = 40$ ms.

$$simulation\ time = \frac{sample\ time}{q} \qquad (1)$$

7 Evaluation

There is no "gold standard" with which to evaluate the operation of simulations (MABS or otherwise). However, the simulation should be as realistic as possible. The mechanism adopted with respect to the work presented in this paper was that the operation of the simulations should be compared with the original video data. Consequently we could compare the distribution of MPs in the simulated data with those produced using the real video data. In the case of the relative mechanism the comparison was conducted by comparing the number of occasions that each MP was recorded with respect to the simulation and video data. However, in the case of the absolute mechanism there were too many locations to provide a meaningful comparison. Recall that the grid size used for the video data was 14×14, thus we had 196 unique locations. Thus, for the absolute analysis we divided the environment into 7×7 blocks, each block representing $2 \times 2 = 4$ "standard" grid cells. As a result 49 blocks were used for the comparison. For each block of cells, the occurrences count of the number of times that an agent visited the block was determined both with respect to the video and simulation data. For the evaluation two scenarios similar to those shown in Figs. 1 and 2, featuring two agents, were used. Both the relative and absolute representations were considered, with and without the concept of states.

The results for the evaluation using absolute MPs are presented in Figs. 5, 6, 7 and 8. Figures 5 and 6 give the results using coarse block grids for videos 1 and 2 using absolute movement patterns without states, while Figs. 7 and 8 present the results for the same videos using absolute movement patterns with states. In each case, the blue bar indicates the occurrence counts extracted from the video data while the red bar the occurrence counts for the simulation. From the figures it can clearly be observed that the behaviour of the mice agents in the simulation is similar to that featured within the video data. We can place a

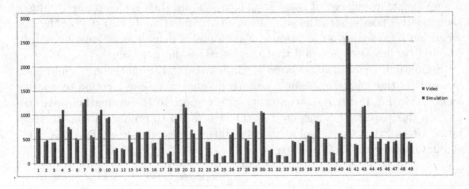

Fig. 5. Comparison of simulation data with video data in terms of blocks visited using absolute MPs without states and video 1

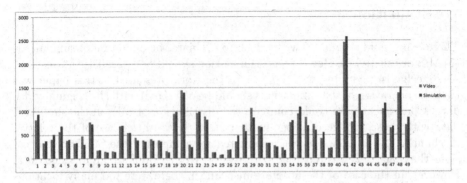

Fig. 6. Comparison of simulation data with video data in terms of blocks visited using absolute MPs without states video 2

value on the "similarity" (sim) of a simulated scenario compared with a real life
scenario, given a set of simulated occurrence counts $F_s = \{s_1, s_2, \dots\}$ and a set
of real occurrence counts $F_r = \{r_1, r_2, \dots\}$, using:

$$sim = \frac{\sum_{i=1}^{i=|F_s|} s_i \sim r_i}{|F_s|} \tag{2}$$

The similarity value obtained using absolute addressing and no states for Video 1
was 0.08 and for Video 2 was 0.11, and when using states the accuracies obtained
were 0.12 and 0.13 respectively (note that ab accuracy of 0.0).

For the evaluation using relative movement patterns, with and without states,
the environment featured 109 relative addresses (location descriptors). If we
include states we have 109 × 4 state-address combinations. Too many to present
in bar graph form (and in this case it did not make sense to consider a coarse
grid as in the case of the absolute addressing evaluation presented above).
A fragment of the results obtained are presented in Tables 1 and 2. The tables list
location descriptors on the left, followed by the difference in occurrence counts

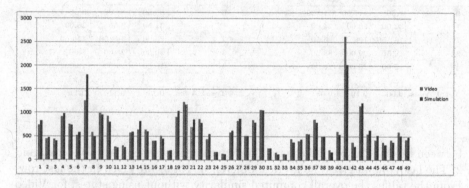

Fig. 7. Comparison of simulation data with video data in terms of blocks visited using
absolute MPs with states and video 1

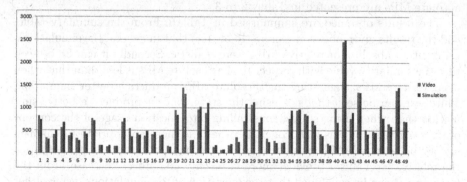

Fig. 8. Comparison of simulation data with video data in terms of blocks visited using
absolute MPs with states and video 2

Table 1. Fragment of differences in recorded frequency counts using relative MPs without states (videos 1 and 2)

Location descriptor	Video 1 diff.	Video 2 diff.	Avg. diff.
wwwoowoow	0.50	1.00	0.75
- - - ssssss	7.00	6.50	6.75
-ss-ss-ss	2.00	3.50	2.75
-ww-wo-wo	7.00	5.00	2.00
oobooowww	5.00	3.00	2.00
...	...	...	...
Total Aves.	0.27	0.21	0.24

Table 2. Fragment of differences in recorded frequency counts using relative MPs with states (videos 1 and 2)

Location descriptor	State	Video 1 diff.	Video 2 diff.	Avg. diff.
- - - ssssss	CloseBy	5.0	3.0	4.0
booboooooo	CloseBy	2.0	2.0	2.0
woossosso	Ignore	2.0	3.0	2.5
woosoosoo	Ignore	4.0	3.0	1.0
ooonoonoo	Ignore	6.0	4.0	2.0
...	...	...	...	...
Total Aves.		0.36	0.30	0.33

Table 3. Fragment of differences in recorded frequency counts using absolute MPs without states (videos 1 and 2)

Block No	Video 1 diff.	Video 2 diff.	Avg. diff.
0	7.50	117.50	110.00
1	32.00	56.00	24.00
2	131.50	106.00	25.50
3	10.50	99.00	88.50
4	15.00	25.00	10.00
...	...	...	...
Total Aves.	0.06	0.10	0.08

Table 4. Fragment of differences in recorded frequency counts using absolute MPs with states (videos 1 and 2)

Block No	Video 1 diff.	Video 2 diff.	Avg. diff.
0	92.50	89.00	3.50
1	31.50	3.50	28.00
2	28.00	144.50	116.50
3	30.00	25.00	5.00
4	10.00	20.00	10.00
...	...	...	...
Total Aves.	0.12	0.11	0.11

between the simulation and the real life experiments as recorded in videos 1 and 2. The last column gives the average difference. Totals are given in the last row. From the tables the overall computed similarity without using states, for Video 1 and 2, was 0.47 and 0.57 respectively; whilst when using states it was 0.58 and 0.62. For completeness fragments of the frequency count results obtained using absolute MPs are presented in Tables 2 to 3.

The results obtained are summarised in Table 5. From the summary table, and the results given above, it can firstly be seen that in general the simulations, using either absolute or relative MPs, were realistic. Secondly it can be be seen that the similarity value with respect to the absolute MPs is less than that when using relative MPs; suggesting that absolute MPs produces a better simulation. Thirdly it can be seen that not using the state concept produces a better simulation than when using states, thus calling into question usage of the concept of states. Overall it was thus concluded that the most appropriate mechanism for our behaviour MABS was the absolute mechanism without states although the relative mechanism provides more versatility. Whatever the case, from the foregoing, it can be concluded that the operation of the simulations, using either absolute or relative MPs, was effective (Table 4).

Table 5. Summary of results

Technique	Ave. diff. Video 1	Ave. diff. Video 2	Net ave. diff. Video. 1 and 2	Sim. Video 1	Sim. video 2	Avr. Sim.
Absolute	0.06	0.10	0.08	0.08	0.11	0.09
Absolute + state	0.11	0.12	0.11	0.12	0.13	0.12
Relative	0.27	0.21	0.24	0.47	0.57	0.52
Relative + state	0.36	0.30	0.33	0.58	0.62	0.60

8   Conclusion

In this paper a process has been introduced for mining Movement Patterns (MPs) from video data in such a way that these can be used in the context of MABS. The idea is to learn the desired MPs from video data, a more efficient and less error prone mechanism than hand crafting. Two mechanism for representing patterns are considered, absolute and relative. Evaluation was conducted by "closing the loop" and comparing the operation of the absolute and relative mechanisms, with and without states, with the original video data. Thus four different representations were considered: (i) absolute with state, (ii) absolute without state, (iii) relative with state and (iv) relative without state. The evaluation indicated that effective simulations were attained, with the absolute representation without states producing the most realistic MABS simulations although with the caveat that relative MPs are more versatile (absolute MPS can only be sed with respect to environments identical to those from which they were generated). For future work, the intention is to consider the proposed mechanism in the context of "many mice" scenarios (more than two) and with respect to other domains.

References

1. Agiriga, E.: A Multi Agent Based Simulation Framework For Mammalian Behaviour. Ph.D. thesis, Department of Computer Science, Univeristy of Liverpool (2016)
2. Agiriga, E., Coenen, F., Hurst, J., Kowalski, D.: A multiagent based framework for the simulation of mammalian behaviour. In: Bramer, M., Petridis, M. (eds.) Research and Development in Intelligent Systems XXX, pp. 435–441. Springer, Cham (2013). doi:10.1007/978-3-319-02621-3_32
3. Bonabeau, E.: Agent-based modeling: methods and techniques for simulating human systems. Proc. Natl. Acad. Sci. **99**(suppl 3), 7280–7287 (2002)
4. Choy, K., Hopgood, A.A., Nolle, L., O'Neill, B.: Implementation of a tileworld testbed on a distributed blackboard system. In: The 18th European Simulation Multiconference (2004)
5. Dumont, B., Hill, D.R.: Multi-agent simulation of group foraging in sheep: effects of spatial memory, conspecific attraction and plot size. Ecol. Model. **141**, 201–215 (2001). Elsevier
6. Klügl, F., Rindsfüser, G.: Large-scale agent-based pedestrian simulation. In: Petta, P., Müller, J.P., Klusch, M., Georgeff, M. (eds.) MATES 2007. LNCS, vol. 4687, pp. 145–156. Springer, Heidelberg (2007). doi:10.1007/978-3-540-74949-3_13

7. Malleson, N., See, L., Evans, A., Heppenstall, A.: Implementing comprehensive offender behaviour in a realistic agent-based model of burglary. Simulation **88**, 50–71 (2010). doi:10.1177/0037549710384124

8. Pan, X., Han, C.S., Dauber, K., Law, K.H.: A multi-agent based framework for the simulation of human and social behaviors during emergency evacuations. AI Soc. **22**, 113–132 (2007). Springer

9. Pavón, J., Gómez-Sanz, J.: Agent oriented software engineering with INGENIAS. In: Multi-Agent Systems and Applications III, pp. 394–403. Springer (2003)

10. Pratt, S.C., Sumpter, D.J., Mallon, E.B., Franks, N.R.: An agent-based model of collective nest choice by the ant Temnothorax albipennis. Anim. Behav. **70**(5), 1023–1036 (2005)

11. Schank, J.C.: The development of locomotor kinematics in neonatal rats: an agent-based modeling analysis in group and individual contexts. J. Theor. Biol. **254**(4), 826–842 (2008)

12. Siebers, P.-O., Aickelin, U.: Introduction to multi-agent simulation (2008)

13. Sun, S., Manson, S.M.: Simple agents, complex emergent city: agent-based modeling of intraurban migration. In: Helbich, M., Jokar Arsanjani, J., Leitner, M. (eds.) Computational Approaches for Urban Environments. GE, vol. 13, pp. 123–147. Springer, Cham (2015). doi:10.1007/978-3-319-11469-9_6

14. Topping, C.J., Hansen, T.S., Jensen, T.S., Jepsen, J.U., Nikolajsen, F., Odderskær, P.: ALMaSS, an agent-based model for animals in temperate european landscapes. Ecol. Model. **167**(1), 65–82 (2003)

15. Tufail, M., Coenen, F., Mu, T., Rind, S.J.: Mining movement patterns from video data to inform multi-agent based simulation. In: Cao, L., Zeng, Y., An, B., Symeonidis, A.L., Gorodetsky, V., Coenen, F., Yu, P.S. (eds.) ADMI 2014. LNCS, vol. 9145, pp. 38–51. Springer, Cham (2015). doi:10.1007/978-3-319-20230-3_4

High-Conductivity Inserts Positioning Approach Using Constructal Theory and Agent-Based Modeling

Paola A. Avendaño[✉], Newton N. Marube, Diana F. Adamatti,
and Jeferson A. Souza

Universidade Federal do Rio Grande, Rio Grande, RS, Brazil
pao.andrea9030@gmail.com

Abstract. Present study addresses a problem of heat transfer by conduction in steady state in which the best geometry (material sites) is
sought in a plate built from two different materials, and subjected to
internal heat generation, such that the resistance to heat flow generated
within it is minimized. An agent-based model developed in NetLogo using
the Constructal Theory is presented. Results show complex geometries
that were compared with other works, finding that using the Constructal Theory, it is possible to obtain close to the optimal geometries very
similar to the forms found in nature in different flow systems.

Keywords: Agent-based simulation · Constructal Theory · Optimization · Heat transfer

1 Introduction

In recent years, engineering problems related to heat transfer have received great
attention. Heat transfer is a dominant aspect in almost all conservation, production and energy conversion devices. An example of this are the advanced studies
to increase the efficiency of a gas turbine engine and to study the efficiency of
a fuel cell. Computational Science, has made possible important discoveries via
advances in thermal engineering that seek to ensure precise control of temperatures in systems covering nanoscale sizes in integrated circuits, micro scale storage media, including compact discs to large data centers full of heat dissipating
equipment, making it possible to keep the operating temperature values of the
devices fairly low so as to ensure their reliable operation. Similarly, heat transfer
plays a critical role in reducing operating temperatures of parts inside personal
computers. Heat transfer is not only important in systems engineering, but also
in nature, being the basis for advancement in biomedical engineering [7]. The
goal of many of these works focuses on explaining how the geometries inside the
solid surfaces studied, influence the performance of heat transfer and, in addition
to understanding, seek to improve their performance and find new geometries

© Springer International Publishing AG 2017
L.G. Nardin and L. Antunes (Eds.): MABS 2016, LNAI 10399, pp. 141–153, 2017.
DOI: 10.1007/978-3-319-67477-3_8

due to the importance to various applications such as heat exchangers, internal combustion engines, electric motors and thermal conductors [2,11,15].

The Constructal Theory, is becoming a powerful methodology, since it sets out to explain the trend of flow throughout nature objects through paths that offer the least "resistance". It is a physical principle that unites animate and inanimate flow systems [4–6]. Being a general theory, this can be applied in all areas where there is some kind of evolution. Thus, it has been used to solve biological, physical, social organizations, technological change, sustainability and engineering problems, among others [6].

Despite the fact that there are numerous studies on the optimization of plates subjected to some heat source, no related work approaches this using agent-based modeling. In agent-based simulation, the individual agents, which can be molecules, cells, trees or consumers in the model are directly represented and have an internal state and set of behaviors or rules that determine how the state of the agent is updated from one time-step to the next [3].

Some studies have developed solutions to minimize the thermal resistance in a low conductivity volumes with heat generation, through construction or optimization of high conductivity channels connected to a heat sink. Beján [4] presents complex forms (assemblies) obtained by combining the optimized elemental geometry to form the final forms after a sequence of optimization and organization steps. The paths form a tree-like network, in which every single geometric detail is determined theoretically is shown. Ledezma, Bejan and Errera [8] present a solution that is built covering the volume with high conductivity blocks that are assembled in sequence. The distribution of the material also resulted in tree-like geometries. In [1], Almogbel and Bejan report two methods to improve the Constructal method used in [8], in which more degrees of freedom are used to define the geometry of the high conductivity path. They can construct highly conductive tree forms which are similar to the shapes seen in nature. Lorenzini et al. [10] applied Constructal Design to discover the configuration that eases the access of the heat that flows through X-shaped pathways of high-conductivity material. Souza and Ordonez [12], for example, propose an optimization algorithm based on the Constructal Theory to find an optimized geometry in which the temperature gradients of low conductivity volumes were calculated and these volumes were replaced with high conductivity material. The geometries that were found in simulations have tree-like similarity. They concluded that the results obtained depend both on the number of replaced volumes in each time increment, as well as the ratio of conductivity of material. In Lorenzini et al. [9], genetic algorithms are used in combination with the Constructal Design to optimize the geometry of an isothermal cavity in "Y" within a conductive plate with the same objective as the previously cited works.

Our approach combines Constructal Theory and Agent-Based Modeling in order to solve the heated optimization problem of how to best positioning high-conductivity inserts inside a base low-conductivity material.

2   Theoretical Framework

This section summarizes all physical principals used to formulate the problem.

2.1   Heat Conduction Problem and the Finite Volume Discretization

This paper presents a problem of steady state conduction heat transfer, where a solid two-dimensional square plate, built from two different materials, one of high and the other of low thermal conductivity. Heat generation is applied to the low thermal conductivity material at a uniform volumetric flow rate (q'''). The solid has completely isolated borders and a heat sink on a border which is maintained at a temperature (T_{min}), thus the heat generated is removed through the high conductivity pathway.

Heat conduction is the transfer of energy that occurs due to the interaction between molecules (collisions), driven by a temperature gradient. One of the main objectives of heat conduction analysis is to determine the temperature field in a medium resulting from the conditions imposed on its borders. That is, one wishes to know the temperature distribution, which represents the variation in temperature relative to the position in the medium.

Equation (1) is a 2D general form in Cartesian coordinates and steady state condition, for the equation of heat conduction in a solid. This equation, commonly called the heat equation, provides the basic tool for the analysis perfomed in this work. From its solution, one can obtain the temperature distribution $T(x, y)$ as a function of position [7]

$$k\frac{\partial^2 T}{\partial x^2} + k\frac{\partial^2 T}{\partial y^2} + q''' = 0 \tag{1}$$

where: T is the temperature (K), t is the time (s), x and y are the Cartesian coordinates (m) and k is the thermal conductivity (W/mK).

Finite Differences Method (FDM), Finite Volumes Method (FVM) and Finite Element Method (FEM) are traditional methods used for the numeric solution of differential equations.

The Finite Volumes Method is used in the present study for the solution of Eq. (1). Figure 1 presents the discretization for an internal volume of the plate in part (a) and the energy balance for the same point in part (b).

With $\Delta x = \Delta y$ and $\Delta z = 1$, the energy balance for a two-dimensional heat transfer problem in steady state is given by:

$$(q''_w - q''_e)\Delta y + (q''_n - q''_s)\Delta x + q'''(\Delta x)^2 = 0 \tag{2}$$

which may be discretized with the FVM [14] resulting in:

$$k_e T_E + k_w T_W + k_n T_N + k_s T_S - (k_w + k_e + k_n + k_s)T_P + q'''(\Delta x)^2 = 0 \tag{3}$$

where the small latter subscripts indicate the volume boundaries (Fig. 1a) and the capital latter subscripts indicate the storage of the variable in the center of the volume.

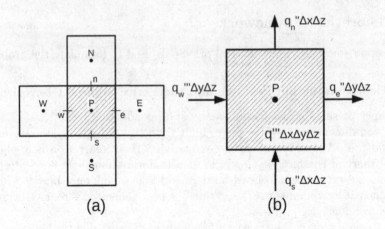

Fig. 1. Energy flow balance

2.2   Constructal Theory

Constructal Theory accounts for the universal tendency of finite flow systems to morph into evolving configurations that provide greater and easier access over time [5,6]. The Constructal tries resolve the many and contradictory ad hoc statements of "optimality" and design, and destiny in nature, such as minimum and maximum entropy production and minimum and maximum flow resistance, and also explains the designs that are observed and copied in biomimetics [12].

Many studies related to heat transfer have been developed using the logic proposed by the Constructal Theory and various optimization methods, but none was found when it comes to the use of agent-based modeling.

The main goal of this work is to determine the appropriate locations for the high and low conductivity materials that form the plate so as to minimize the maximum interior temperature of the plate. Figure 2 shows the boundary conditions used and a possible configuration for the problem, where the gray region is the high conductivity material and the white region is the low conductivity material in the plate.

According to the Constructal Design, the search for the best location of the material k_p within the plate, is subject to two restrictions that are the total area occupied by the plate given by:

$$A = H \times L \tag{4}$$

where H and L are the length and width, and the area occupied by the high conductivity material, that is:

$$A_p = H_0 \times L_0 \tag{5}$$

The Eqs. 4 and 5 can be written as the fraction

$$\phi = \frac{A_p}{A} \tag{6}$$

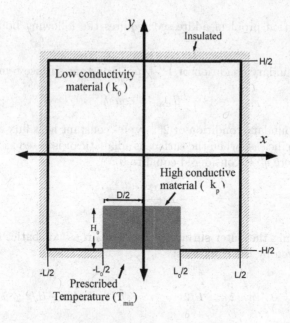

Fig. 2. Problem description

The analysis used to calculate the dimensionless heat resistance as a function of the geometry consists in numerically solving Eq. (7) over the low conductivity region where heat generation occurs [12]:

$$k_0 \frac{\partial^2 \theta}{\partial \tilde{x}^2} + k_0 \frac{\partial^2 \theta}{\partial \tilde{y}^2} + \frac{1}{1-\phi} = 0 \tag{7}$$

and Eq. (8) over the high conductivity region:

$$k_p \frac{\partial^2 \theta}{\partial \tilde{x}^2} + k_p \frac{\partial^2 \theta}{\partial \tilde{y}^2} = 0 \tag{8}$$

where: k_0 will be used to represent the conductivities of low conductivity material, k_p to represent the conductivities of high conductivity material and the dimensionless variables are:

$$\theta = \frac{(T - T_{min})W}{q_0/k_0} \tag{9}$$

$$(\tilde{x}, \tilde{y}) = \frac{(x, y)}{A^{(1/2)}}, \quad \phi = \frac{A_p}{A} \tag{10}$$

The dimensionless thermal resistance is defined by:

$$\theta_{max} = \frac{(T_{max} - T_{min})W}{q_0/k_0} \tag{11}$$

The conduction problem addressed requires the following boundary conditions:

– Dirichlet boundary condition or 1st-type - constant surface temperature:

$$T_{min} = const \tag{12}$$

– Neumann boundary condition or 2nd-type - constant heat flux on the surface (being a specific case when the surface is adiabatic or isolated as in the current problem where q'' is considered equal to 0):

$$-k \left. \frac{\partial T}{\partial x} \right|_{x-l} = q'' \tag{13}$$

Thus, defining the outer surface of the domain as adiabatic, the boundary condition is given by the equations:

$$\frac{\partial \theta}{\partial \tilde{x}} = 0 \quad in \quad \tilde{x} = -\tilde{L}/2 \quad or \quad \tilde{x} = \tilde{L}/2 \quad and \quad -\tilde{H}/2 \leq \tilde{y} \leq \tilde{H}/2 \tag{14}$$

$$\frac{\partial \theta}{\partial \tilde{y}} = 0 \quad in \quad \tilde{y} = \tilde{H}/2 \quad and \quad -\tilde{L}/2 \leq \tilde{x} \leq \tilde{L}/2 \tag{15}$$

$$\frac{\partial \theta}{\partial \tilde{y}} = 0 \quad in \quad \tilde{y} = -\tilde{H}/2 \quad and \quad -\tilde{L}/2 \leq \tilde{x} \leq -\tilde{L}_0/2 \quad or \quad \tilde{L}_0/2 \leq \tilde{x} \leq \tilde{L}/2 \tag{16}$$

3   Proposed Model

Agent based modeling is often used in complex systems. It considers that simple and complex phenomena can be the result of interactions between autonomous and independent entities, which operate within systems in accordance with different modes of interaction [3]. In Netlogo can be found a Heat diffusion model which simulates transient and steady-state temperature distribution, of a thin plate. Agent-based modeling is used in the heat diffusion model to illustrate the time dependent emergence observed during simulation. As the simulation runs, heat is transmitted from warmer parts of the plate to cooler parts of the plate as shown by the varying color of the plate. Therefore, the temperature of the plate begins to change immediately and possibly differently at different locations, gradually converging to a stable state [13]. However, the model proposed in this work has great differences with respect to the mentioned model. This is because in present work it is not only necessary to reach a stable state. The plate presented here has totally different boundary conditions, it is constructed with different conductive materials and the aim of the work is to construct pathways of the high-conductivity material, thus, it was necessary to develop a new model.

NetLogo is a programming language useful for the simulation of various social phenomena, particularly for the simulation of complex problems that evolve over time.

Within the programming environment there are hundreds or thousands of elements called "agents", which, independently, can receive instructions or store information that is offered by the modeler, which makes it possible to subtract, at every iteration, different types of global and/or punctual information [13].

Thus, an agent-based model that uses Constructal Theory was developed for the search for optimal positions of high conductivity material in the plate.

To achieve the objective of the work, one must first divide the computational domain into small volumes (agents), all with low thermal conductivity and calculate the temperature field using the Finite Volumes Method. After reaching the steady state solution (when temperature change from one iteration to another becomes negligible) a group of volumes of low conductivity, k_0, and located in the region of higher temperature gradient are, replaced by high conductivity, k_p, material. The replacement process should be repeated until the amount of high conductivity material made available to the problem is used. Figure 3 shows an example of how the sequential replacement process occurs. In this case, it is a plate with 81 volumes, in which two low thermal conductivity volumes are replaced by two high-conductivity volumes at each iteration until a plate having 30% k_p material is reached.

Figure 3 (a) shows the computational domain with all volumes having low conductivity (gray color). Figure 3 (b) show the location of the high conductivity materials (red color) after the first iteration in which 2 volumes were replaced, Fig. 3 (c) shows the geometry of the high conductive material after substitution of 8 volumes (four time steps). Figure 3 (d) shows the configuration obtained after replacing 24 volumes which correspond to 30% of the material.

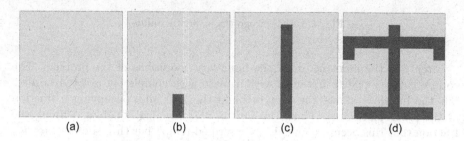

(a)   (b)   (c)   (d)

Fig. 3. The replacement process (Color figure online)

The pseudo-algorithm proposed is shown below:
1: Make the discretization of the computational domain into small volumes.
2: Define: set the boundary conditions of the problem, k_p/k_0, ϕ, k_p, N_c.
3: **for all** (x,y) in the domain **do**
4:     $Conductivity[(x, y)] = k_0$

5: **while** $(A_p/A < \phi)$ **do**
6:    Calculate the temperature range of the plate
7:    Sort all volumes with $Conductivity[(x,y)]$ $=$ k_0 according to $max(dT/dx, dT/dy)$
8:    Create a list with the N_c volumes with $max(dT/dx, dT/dy)$.
9:    **for** i=1:N_c **do**
10:       Assign $Conductivity[(x,y)] = k_p$ for the i-th element of the above list

Figure 4 shows the GUI of the developed model in which one can observe the simulation in progress. According to the proposed pseudo-algorithm, grid refinement should be done and each "patch" (NetLogo graphic unit) within the interface is a grid element.

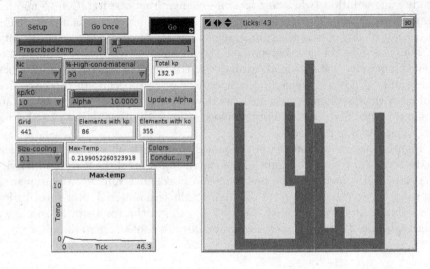

Fig. 4. GUI Netlogo (Color figure online)

Step 2 is the moment to set the boundary conditions of the problem. The code was developed to initialize with a plate with completely isolated borders but the interface allows the user to build the heat sink occupying a fraction of the lower plate area. Thus, the button "Size-cooling" enables defining the fraction that this occupies and the "Prescribed-temp" bar the temperature (K) in which it is kept. In addition, at this stage the following variables must be set: the number of volumes that will be replaced at each iteration ("N_c" button); the overall percentage of high conductivity material that will be placed on the plate ("%-High-cond-material" button) which is calculated as the number of volumes and displayed on the screen "Total k_p"; and the ratio between the conductivities of the materials (k_p/k_0 button). After choosing the relationship between the two materials, simply click the "Update Alpha" button and the conductivity value of the materials will be restarted (another option is to change the value of the conductivities ratio directly to the desired value). One can also choose the way in which the simulation can be visualized using colors for each conductivity, color gradient based on the temperature or color gradient based on the maximum temperature gradient ("Colors" button).

During the third and fourth step, a low conductivity (k_0) is assigned to all volumes of the grid and from *step 6* the temperature field in the computational domain is calculated using the Finite Volumes Method. After reaching the steady state, the amount of low conductivity volumes "N_c" that present the highest temperatures gradients must be replaced by high-conductivity material. The monitors "Grid", "Elements with k_p", "Elements with k_0" e "Max-temp" make it possible to follow a simulation in the same manner as maximum temperature graph. Procedure from *Step 6* is repeated until the total amount of material is inserted.

4   Results

Some of the characteristics of the plates will be kept invariant during all simulations, so the results presented in this section correspond to the plates that have the following parameters in common:

- $H \times L = 1$
- $H \cdot L = 1$
- $D = 0.1$
- $q''' = 1$

The number of volumes that the plate is divided influences the numerical solution approximation of the temperature field. Fine tuning is critical to the efficiency of the method because the solution involves differential equations. Thus, by varying the number of volumes in which the plate is divided, the best results may be obtained. The first part shows simulations for a plate divided into 961 volumes (31×31). In this case, the influence of N_c while obtaining geometries is studied. Thus, five simulations are carried out maintaining $\phi = 0.1$, $k_p/k_0 = 5$ fixed and varying the N_c. Results of maximum temperature for each case are shown in Table 1.

Table 1. Influence of N_c on the results. $\phi = 0.1$, $k_p/k_0 = 5$, Grid=961 volumes

Nc	θ_{max}
1	0.5573
2	0.4572
5	0.46
10	0.4607
25	0.4692

From Fig. 5 geometries formed by highly conductive paths can be observed. These were formed after applying the methodology with the plate characteristics described above. The geometry that offered lower resistance to heat flow was constructed using $N_c = 2$.

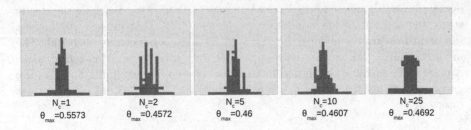

$N_c=1$ $\theta_{max}=0.5573$ $N_c=2$ $\theta_{max}=0.4572$ $N_c=5$ $\theta_{max}=0.46$ $N_c=10$ $\theta_{max}=0.4607$ $N_c=25$ $\theta_{max}=0.4692$

Fig. 5. Geometries corresponding to the values shown in Table 1

From the analysis for Fig. 5 it is possible observe that, the greater the amount of information that is exchanged at each iteration, the higher the maximum temperature which occurs in the computational domain, i.e., less optimized is the solution.

Using information from Table 1 and Fig. 5, future simulations will be carried out using $N_c = 2$. Now, aiming to obtain a numerical solution with best approach, the mesh used is finer, having 1681 square volumes (41 × 41). Thus, results obtained using different values for the thermal conductivity of the high conductivity material and different amounts of the inserts are summarized in Table 2 and graphically represented in Fig. 6.

Table 2. Summmary of the θ_{max} values obtained

ϕ	k_p/k_0			
	5	10	100	300
0.05	0.4865	0.3781	0.1522	0.1069
0.1	0.4138	0.2971	0.0272	0.0139
0.2	0.3644	0.2285	0.0038	0.0041
0.3	0.3736	0.2115	0.0021	0.002

Figure 6 (a) shows the behavior of θ_{max} for different values of ϕ. The greater the amount of high conductivity material used, the better the imperfections are distributed. In (b), one can observe the behavior of θ_{max} dependent on the amount of material of the type k_p used. When ϕ is greater than 20%, the θ_{max} decreases by an average of 46 times when increasing the thermal conductivity of $k_p = 5-100$, but when the same thermal conductivity increases by $k_p = 100-300$ the minimal dimensionless maximal excess of temperture is only 1.5 times better, which becomes important data for the experimental case.

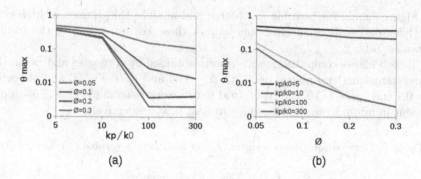

(a)   (b)

Fig. 6. Influence of k_p/k_0 and ϕ in the value of θ_{max}

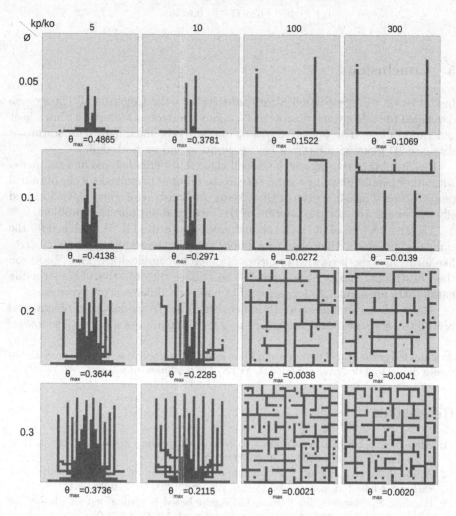

Fig. 7. Final geometry obtained for the combination of various ϕ and k_p/k_0

Figure 7 makes it possible to observe and analyze the settings of high conductivity paths obtained after simulations, those corresponding to the results shown in Table 2.

Table 3 allows comparisons with results obtained by Almogbel and Bejan [1]. Thus, comparing two plates, one with $\phi = 0.05$ and $k_p/k_0 = 300$ and one with $\phi = 0.1$ and $k_p/k_0 = 10$, those obtained in this work were 35.6% and 22.5% more efficient in minimizing the resistance to heat flow, respectively.

Table 3. Comparison between current result and those presented in reference [1]

Φ	k_p/k_0	This work	Reference [1]
0.05	300	0.1069	0.145
0.1	10	0.2971	0.3640

5   Conclusions

In this work, an agent-based algorithm that uses the Constructal Theory was developed to seek optimal positions of a highly conductive material within a heat generation plate. The objective was to minimize the maximum temperature of a square 2D plate with internal heat generation and on heat skin.

Results obtained using the developed algorithm were analyzed and compared with other results, showing a coherence in the order of magnitude of the obtained temperatures Thus, it is evident that the use of Constructal Theory provides and efficient alternative for the solution of the presented optimization problem.

The architecture of the high conductivity paths proved to be branched for the simulated problems, thus observing among some of the resulting geometry, treelike forms in structures with branches of different complexities. Thus, based on the Constructal Theory, it was possible to achieve the objective of constructing paths thats are similar to forms found in nature in different flow systems.

The NetLogo simulation environment was used to model the problem, and proved to be a powerful development tool for simulation of natural phenomena.

Acknowledgements. The author acknowledges the Coordenação de Aperfeicionamento de Pessoal de Nível Superior (CAPES) for the financial support.

References

1. Almogbel, M., Bejan, A.: Conduction trees with spacings at the tips. Int. J. Heat Mass Transf. **42**(20), 3739–3756 (1999)
2. Azad, A.V., Amidpour, M.: Economic optimization of shell and tube heat exchanger based on constructal theory. Energy **36**(2), 1087–1096 (2011)
3. Bandini, S., Manzoni, S., Vizzari, G.: Agent based modeling and simulation: an informatics perspective. J. Artif. Soc. Soc. Simul. **12**(4), 4 (2009)

4. Bejan, A.: Constructal-theory network of conducting paths for cooling a heat generating volume. Int. J. Heat Mass Transf. **40**(4), 799–816 (1997)
5. Bejan, A.: Shape and Structure, from Engineering to Nature. Cambridge University Press, Cambridge (2000)
6. Bejan, A., Zane, J.P.: Design in nature. Mech. Eng. **134**(6), 42 (2012)
7. Bergman, T.L., Incropera, F.P., Lavine, A.S.: Fundamentals of Heat and Mass Transfer. John Wiley & Sons, New Jersey (2011)
8. Ledezma, G., Bejan, A., Errera, M.: Constructal tree networks for heat transfer. J. Appl. Phys. **82**(1), 89–100 (1997)
9. Lorenzini, G., Biserni, C., Estrada, E.D.S.D., DOS Santos, E.D., Isoldi, L.A., Rocha, L.A.O.: Genetic algorithm applied to geometric optimization of isothermal y-shaped cavities. J. Electron. Packag. **136**(3), 031011 (2014)
10. Lorenzini, G., Biserni, C., Rocha, L.A.O.: Constructal design of x-shaped conductive pathways for cooling a heat-generating body. Int. J. Heat Mass Transf. **58**(1), 513–520 (2013)
11. Lorenzini, G., Estrada, E.D.S.D., Dos Santos, E.D., Isoldi, L.A., Rocha, L.A.O.: Constructal design of convective cavities inserted into a cylindrical solid body for cooling. Int. J. Heat Mass Transf. **83**, 75–83 (2015)
12. Souza, J.A., Ordonez, J.C.: Constructal design of high-conductivity inserts. In: Rocha, L., Lorente, S., Bejan, A. (eds.) Constructal Law and the Unifying Principle of Design. UCS. Springer, New York (2013). doi:10.1007/978-1-4614-5049-8_6
13. Tisue, S., Wilensky, U.:. Netlogo: a simple environment for modeling complexity. In: International Conference on Complex Systems, Boston, MA, vol. 21 (2004)
14. Versteeg, H.K., Malalasekera, W.: An Introduction to Computational Fluid Dynamics: The Finite Volume Method. Pearson Education, London (2007)
15. Yang, J., Fan, A., Liu, W., Jacobi, A.M.: Optimization of shell-and-tube heat exchangers conforming to tema standards with designs motivated by constructal theory. Energy Convers. Manage. **78**, 468–476 (2014)

Author Index

Printed in the United States
By Bookmasters